Date Due

BRODART   CAT. NO. 23 233   PRINTED IN U.S.A.

WHAT MUST THE CHURCH DO?

CONTENTS

FOREWORD

In the original plan for "The Interseminary Series," it was proposed that a brief concluding volume, attempting to draw into summary the major findings of the preceding four symposia, should be written by the chairman of the Interseminary Committee; and the series was so announced.

Two factors have necessitated an alteration in this plan. On the one hand, unforeseen calls have taken the chairman of the Interseminary Committee to the Orient and to Europe in the weeks which had been reserved for writing, and it has been impossible for him to fulfill the assignment. On the other hand, it was increasingly obvious that no one was so well equipped to write the summarizing volume as the secretary of the Interseminary Committee who had guided the four earlier volumes through every stage of their preparation. Accordingly, a scheme of joint authorship was determined upon; the secretary would prepare a preliminary draft of the concluding book, and the chairman would whip it into final shape.

However, when Mr. Bilheimer presented his manuscript for revision, another alteration in plan was clearly indicated. What had been expected to be merely a preliminary draft was a finished work. I have been able to suggest only such minor changes as any friendly critic of a manuscript would propose. This book is wholly Mr. Bilheimer's.

It is altogether appropriate that this concluding number in
"The Interseminary Series" should come from his pen alone.
It was he who first conceived the idea of a great interseminary
conference to be preceded by two years of preparatory study.
It was he who projected "The Interseminary Series" as a
principal instrument of preparation. His mind has fathered
the scheme at every point. His vision and spirit have claimed
the enthusiastic participation of a remarkably able company
of collaborators. As painstaking and tireless editor of the series,
he has directed what might have been a group of disconnected
essays into a high degree of unity. And now he has crowned
this effort by giving us a book which, despite its small com-
pass, indeed partly because of its admirable succinctness, may
well take a place among the most valuable on the steadily
lengthening shelf of the chronicles of contemporary ecumenical
Christianity.

In behalf of the Interseminary Committee and also of those
who have shared in this exciting project in co-operative authorship of "The Interseminary Series," I welcome this opportunity
to pay a tribute of admiration and gratitude to one who has
brought the Interseminary Movement to new birth, and who has
kindled the imaginations of increasing numbers of American
theological students and professors with conviction of the
possibilities and claims of the "Ecumenical Reformation." It
now remains for the faculties and student bodies of our semin-
aries to bring these plans to worthy fulfillment in the National
Interseminary Conference of June, 1947.

HENRY P. VAN DUSEN
Chairman, The Interseminary Committee

August 22, 1946

PREFACE

THE INTERSEMINARY SERIES

The five volumes which comprise "The Interseminary Series" have three main purposes: to outline the character of the contemporary world which challenges the Church; to proclaim afresh the nature of the Gospel and the Church which must meet that challenge; and to set forth the claims which ecumenical Christianity makes upon the various churches as they face their world task. Although the perspective of the volumes is American, it is nevertheless comprehensive in that it views the Church as the Body of Christ in the world, performing a mission to the whole world.

The immediate occasion for the publication of the series is a national conference of theological students scheduled for June, 1947, under the auspices and initiative of the Interseminary Movement in the United States. The volumes will serve as study material for the delegates to the conference.

From the outset, however, it has been the desire and aim of those sponsoring the project that the volumes have a wide appeal. They have been designed for the Christian public in general, in the hope that there may be in them help toward our common Christian task in the fateful postwar days.

To produce the volumes, the Interseminary Committee outlined the five major questions and organized the Commissions which are listed below. Each Commission met once, and in the course of a two-day meeting outlined, first, the chapters for its respective volume, and, second, the main elements to be contained in each chapter. Authors were assigned from within the Commission. A first draft of each paper was submitted to Commission members and the chairman of the Commission for criticism, returned and subsequently rewritten in final form. It should be specially noted that the work of Commission I-B was graciously undertaken by the already organized Pacific Coast Theological Group to which were added a few guests for the purpose at hand.

The volumes thus represent a combination of group thinking and individual effort. They are not designed to be completely representative statements to which the Commissions, or the Interseminary Movement, would subscribe. They are intended, rather, to convey information and to stimulate thought, in the earnest hope that this may in turn contribute to a more faithful performance of our Christian mission in the world.

The Foreword generously states the process by which the authorship of the present volume was determined, and indicates the extent of the debt by virtue of which the author has been able to proceed at all. Not only for many criticisms as to wording and content, but also for suggestions as to the overall structure of the ensuing chapters, as well as for ever gracious and wise leadership throughout the development of the entire project, the author is indebted to Dr. Van Dusen in a way which cannot be fully acknowledged.

As the concluding volume of the series, it was intended that much of its content be taken from the preceding volumes. The footnotes in the text indicate the individual sources, but a general indebtedness to the combined efforts of the authors, the members of the Commissions and particularly the editors of the separate volumes must here be gratefully acknowledged. Particular reference must be made to the indispensable counsel of Professor Latourette, from the beginning stages of the entire project through the completion of the present volume. It need hardly be added that in spite of heavy drawing from many sources, the author alone is responsible for the book.

Robert S. Bilheimer

1

THE ESSENCE OF THE CHALLENGE

1. The characteristics of the age: obsession with economic achievement; the dominance of groups, and their rivalry for power; the substitution of a mechanical for a spiritual unity; personal tensions leading toward disastrous rather than creative life. 2. The challenge to Christianity: denial of man's full stature; the aim of Christianity; the vital conflict.

WHAT is the challenge which faces the Church? Not so long ago, fierce persecution threatened its existence in Continental Europe. Revolutions which are unseating the cultures of centuries sweep the Oriental lands, all but engulfing the tiny Christian communities there. Vast forces are amassed in formations which leave little room for true religion and which relegate the Church to a seat on the sidelines. Large increases in church membership in the United States are so corroded by complacent indifference that they seem to have little more than a statistical significance. The Church itself, in this country and in others, seems almost to fear the power of its own message, and hangs back, weakened by divisions of race, of class, of belief, of vested interest. What is the challenge?

THE CHARACTERISTICS OF THE AGE

In seeking an answer, we shall be largely concerned with the American scene, conscious, however, that this is vitally

1

affected by the tides of world cultural development. We shall proceed not by the analysis of historical causes which have led us to our present condition, but rather by a description of those elements in society which appear to be dominant in our time. Of these there are four:

(1) *An obsession with economic achievement.* It is perfectly true that a large part of men's energies must be spent in securing economic goods, and that in turn the production and distribution of them, together with the financing of the whole economic structure, consume an even greater portion of man's effort. This, as is so often and rightly noted, is part of life itself. It is not necessary to follow Karl Marx and his philosophical descendents in their theory that all of life is determined by economic wants and efforts to satisfy them, to give due and serious recognition to the fact that these are a fundamental part of human existence.

Economic life, however, has become an obsession for our society. The importance of money alone is sufficient to establish the fact. Conventional thinking habitually defines success in life in terms of money and the things money will buy. First impressions of "how well along" a person is are generally registered in terms of his house, his car, how much he is "worth."

> Money today is a symbol of the Good, and to acquire money is to acquire the Good as to lose it is to lose the Good. There is no commandment greater than "Thou shalt acquire money." The most convincing sign of superiority among us is wealth.[1]

[1] Joseph Haroutunian, "Men among Machines," in Clarence Tucker Craig, ed., *The Challenge of Our Culture*, Vol. I of "The Interseminary Series" (New York: Harper & Brothers, 1946), p. 16. Hereafter reference to "The Interseminary Series" will be by author, volume and page only.

It is hardly necessary to point out the symbolic importance of money: it is that which makes available to us the varied resources of economic life, goods and the power to control goods. The importance attached to money indicates the hold which economic activity has over our lives.

There is a special reason for this obsession of our time. Although men have always had to strive for the things of life and have valued them highly, a new factor has entered our scene which has meant that a normal concern has become magnified out of all proportion. This is the fact that it is possible, through the machine and all that it means for production, *indefinitely to gratify the desire of all men for comfort and power.* Prior to the advent of mechanized production, it was possible to produce goods only in limited quantities, and standards of living, measured in terms of the amounts of goods available, were low. Moreover, the firms and agencies (with few exceptions) engaged in the production of goods were in turn limited, and men were not able to gain far-reaching economic power over others. The industrial revolution, however, wrought change at just these points. Machines made it possible to produce in unlimited quantities; the vast combinations of machines needed for such massive production made necessary the concentrations of economic power, so marked in our society. If one grant that there is imbedded in the human ego a twofold desire for comfortable well being and for power,[2] it is clear that in the indefinite gratification of these which the machine makes possible there is the chief

[2] For an extended discussion of these factors in human nature, see Philip Leon, *The Ethics of Power* (London: George Allen & Unwin Ltd., 1935), especially the chapters on "Egoism and Morality" and "Egotism in Itself."

and distinctive cause for our characteristic obsession with economic activity.[3]

Three related factors, however, must be pointed out. The first of these is the excessive stimulation of our desires by modern techniques of advertising. It is conceivable that advertising might be merely an information service, in which firms would tell the public what is available, at what price, and in what places. "Advertising," said Adolph Ochs of the New York *Times,* "is of the very essence of the news. If an advertisement does not give useful and valuable information, the advertiser is wasting his money."[4] How drastically such a concept of advertising cuts across current practice! In the daily newspapers, we find such a service occasionally rendered. But the vast majority of advertising space is used not for information but for stimulation. Advertising is a means of selling, and almost any device is employed. Sex stimulation, gross exaggeration, unremitting repetition, arresting typography and the pleasing use of color, appeals to ambition, play upon natural fear and sympathy and the desire for security, are all used to impress upon us the absolute necessity of possessing everything from cigarettes to automobiles and old-age pensions. It is not enough that machines make possible the surfeit of our natural desires; these in themselves are stimulated to the end that goods are transformed into the Good.

The second factor is the availability of goods. Perhaps in no other country in the world could this be mentioned at the present time as a dominant factor in society. Shortly after the close of World War II, a European youth leader came from

---

[3] For a discussion of the contrast between this desire for indefinite gratification and the desire of other ages for eternity, see Joseph Haroutunian, Vol. I, pp. 19 ff.

[4] Quoted in the New York *Times* Book Review, p. 16, August 18, 1946.

the Continent to this country; his dominant impression upon walking the streets of New York for the first time in a number of years was of the multiplicity of things which crowded the store windows. This experience establishes the point. America was left intact, not robbed of machinery, and she alone is a land of plenty. The entire world is potentially so, because the machine and the complex and ingenious uses to which we have learned to put it can provide us with an unlimited quantity of goods. Though these may for reasons of maldistribution not be immediately within reach of many, they are nevertheless there. They mock those who cannot afford them; they fill the houses of those who can. We are obsessed with economic activity because, in large part, of the unlimited quantities of goods which are available.

More basically, however, this obsession fills our minds because of the motive upon which our economic structure is built. We are driven by the necessities of competition. Though the actual area in which genuine competition is possible may be increasingly limited by growing monopoly,[5] this is the dominant motive, even for the development of centralized control. It is a motive which calls forth the entire energies of the firm and the individual. It commands loyalty to the company; it demands unceasing striving to outdo the competitors. It stimulates advertising; it makes necessary new inventions, both of new machines for the production of new goods, and of improved methods in order that the product may be turned out more quickly, in greater quantity and more cheaply. With the effectiveness of the principle of competition as a governing force for the economic system we are not concerned. It is clear, however, that competition lies close to the root of our obsession with economic processes. Its ceaseless demands give no moment

[5] Elmer J. F. Arndt, Vol. I., pp. 53 ff.

of rest, but urge constantly on toward more production, more selling, more financing—in short, toward more economic activity.

(2) *The dominance of groups, and their rivalry for power.* Our society has seen the emergence of conscious groups of all types, and is now the field in which they strive with one another for the possession of power. This group consciousness, indeed, is one of the characteristic features of our age. It appears in two forms: organized groups and those which, although they are highly self-conscious, are nevertheless unorganized.

Organization is a necessity.

> Individuals, by themselves, are unable to make any appreciable impression upon the social processes of our time. Nothing much can be accomplished in business, or politics, or education, or religion, except by setting in motion forces issuing from the interests and will of organized groups of men.[6]

It is not merely that organization is expedient; the inescapable fact is that it is necessary. As simple an operation as starting a one-man store involves complex organization: the whole line from raw material to finished product on the store shelf is an object lesson in interrelated functions. Beyond this, however, is the fact that power for survival, power for financial success, power for influencing public opinion depend upon organization.

The numbers and types of organizations are legion.[7] Political bodies, ranging from the Lovestoneites to the Republican party,

[6] Joseph Haroutunian, Vol. I, p. 27.
[7] See Randolph Crump Miller, ed., *The Church and Organized Movements*, Vol. II, of "The Interseminary Series," (New York: Harper & Brothers, 1946).

charitable organizations dispersing funds running from dimes to millions, fraternal lodges, educational institutions of all descriptions, religious agencies, all are familiar aspects of contemporary life. There is scarcely a citizen who is not a member of one or more organizations for some specific purpose. Greatest power, and therefore greatest significance, is attached, however, to organizations of certain types. It is evident that more and more the direction of our society turns about three dominant forms: corporations, unions and governments. Here is organization on the grand scale, a scale the very existence of which is evidence of the importance of organization in society. Little is manufactured unless by the giant corporation; the worker stands small chance in his job outside his union; recourse to governmental co-ordination, supervision and control is increasingly necessary for the whole. Here indeed is a dominant element in society today.

The effect of this multiplicity of organization upon the individual is marked. Just as men organize for a particular function, so within the organization the individual has an assigned role.

> Each man has his job, and he is recognized and estimated by it. A man is one who plays this or that role in an organization far greater than himself. The job defines man's *raison d'etre*, and apart from the job he is without value. His private life, his sensibilities and responses, his own personal destiny as well as responsible decisions, as unrelated to his job, are secondary even when consequential. He is a functioning part first, a *person* secondly. He is qualified and disqualified as an instrument rather than as an end.[8]

The real end for hundreds of thousands of people is in the organization. Pride in the firm is consciously developed, and

[8] Joseph Haroutunian, Vol. I, p. 22.

the loyalty which follows from it is regarded as qualification for higher responsibilities. Speaking of labor, Elton Trueblood points out:

> That these men have found an alternative faith cannot reasonably be denied. . . . they have found another gospel. The labor movement now has its own heroes of the faith who are, in many cases, followed with un-questioning loyalty. . . . Though most of the men who make up the rank and file of the labor movement are wholly innocent of conscious doctrine or theory, they are really held together by a kind of truncated idealism.[9]

And the entire world is grievously aware of the powerful temptation to regard the state as an end in itself, worthy of complete loyalty. Organization in our time has come in large part to define the role of the individual, and to supply him with an object of faith and devotion.

Conscious groupings are in evidence not only through or-ganization, but through the "mass mind" as well. This is a men-tality which cannot be associated with any one class of people. "The masses appear wherever the mind of the individual is a simple reflection of the pattern of an organization."[10] The mass mind is an automatic response, to which virtually everyone, in one fashion or another, in our society is subject. The men-tality which views all religion as the opiate of the people, as well as that which regards all men in overalls as representa-tives of the "masses," are equally illustrative of the mass mind.

> When men's judgments are molded by a given news-paper, or advertiser, or radio commentator, or by the higher-ups in an organization, then they belong to the masses. When they reflect the prejudices, tastes, stand-

[9] Elton Trueblood, Vol. II, p. 35.
[10] Joseph Haroutunian, Vol. I, p. 26.

ards, ambitions and responses of a group, they are parts
of a mass. The mass . . . is a group in which private
judgment is suspended.[11]

The most obvious, and disastrous, example of mass mentality
is race prejudice. Here individuals are governed by set atti-
tudes which, as they are passed from person to person and
down through the generations, gather a force of their own.[12]
We are not allowed, except by the most strenuous discipline,
to think through our separate relations with the different races.
We emerge from childhood into a mass mentality which
accepts and vigorously upholds a caste system in which the
white man is on the top and the Negro or other non-Caucasian
is at the bottom. In the face of scientific and cultural evidence
to the contrary, this stereotyped attitude is dominant.

> The individual merely takes over the attitudes and
> stereotypes which prevail in the society into which he is
> born. Race attitudes in contemporary America are formed
> not so much through contacts with other races as through
> contact with prevailing race attitudes. The individual
> learns to react to the symbols of race in terms of the
> patterns of caste, and dynamically in terms of the caste
> struggle.[13]

Here the conscious but unorganized group finds its most dramatic expression. No less than in tangible organization, the
individual is controlled in his thinking and his actions by the
mass mind, and through the operation of it the lives of
thousands of others are molded.

Social groupings would be significant if they could be considered in themselves, that is, statically only; they have, how-

[11] *Ibid.*, p. 26.
[12] Buell G. Gallagher, Vol. I, pp. 96 ff.
[13] *Ibid.*, p. 96.

ever, an even larger significance in the fact that they must also
be regarded dynamically, as centers of power, and the agents
of power rivalries. One cannot survey the contemporary scene
without being impressed with the degree of centralization of
power. Vast organizations in themselves control wide areas
of life; combinations of organizations wield even greater influence. Only fifty-six corporations, for instance, in 1941 held
as much as 75 per cent of all the government orders for
national defense.[14] Here, residing in the hands of but a few
individuals, rested the power of decision, the wisdom of management, and the ability to command the loyalty of the thousands of needed workers upon which, literally, the political
and military fate of a nation depended. This power carries
over into peacetime economy in the form of control over
smaller concerns, through "such policies as 'price leadership,'
'sharing the market,' 'price stabilization,' 'non-price competition,' and the like."[15] The combination of corporations in trade
associations on the national level and in cartels on an international scale further increases this centralization of power.[16]
One notes the same tendency in labor unions. A single union
may run into a membership of hundreds of thousands, and
the combinations of these in both the American Federation of
Labor and the Congress of Industrial Organizations, as well
as in the Railway Brotherhoods, result in power coalitions
which, though they have different purposes, are nevertheless
comparable to those formed by corporations. And these are
typical of massed power in other spheres of life. The modern
nation-state is an aggregate of power, its effectiveness in the
international scene entirely dependent upon the size of the

[14] Elmer J. F. Arndt, Vol. I, p. 54.
[15] *Ibid.*, p. 54.
[16] *Ibid.*, pp. 55-58.

stick it can wield. The age-old self-expansiveness of states has been augmented by two roughly contemporary developments, heightened nationalism and science,[17] which is to say that an initial and inherent impulse to power has been indefinitely extended by the force of a religious faith and the always advancing techniques of industrialism. Here are not only organizations of a scope almost to stagger the imagination, but also an increasing centralization of power which, if uncontrolled for the public good, is the most ominous feature of our time.

The rivalries which are produced are clear and far reaching. As has already been hinted, the struggle for power between corporations and their combinations is a struggle for the control of markets and resources. It is also, and here is the crucial issue for American democracy, a struggle for the control of political power.[18] So great has become the influence of concentrated economic power, that an extension of it further into the political scene through control over government would seriously jeopardize democracy itself.

> For when any group representing a special interest secures a monopoly of political power, the inevitable result is not only the use of the government to promote its own interests at the expense of the welfare of the whole community but also to destroy the means of effective criticism of its use of power.[19]

Labor unions join the rivalry, for in essence they are organizations for the limitation of the control of management, and though there is at present only a beginning of the attempt to enter politics directly, their weight is felt there as well.

[17] See *Ibid.*, pp. 46-47, and Elton Trueblood, Vol. II, pp. 37-38, and 40-42.
[18] Elmer J. F. Arndt, Vol. I, pp. 51-53.
[19] *Ibid.*, p. 52.

Here in the stream of economic and political life is a struggle
for the possession of power, upon the outcome of which the
health of our society depends. It must be noted, also, that this
power rivalry is not confined to organizations as such. The self-
conscious but unorganized groups to which we had reference
are also engaged in strife. The mass mind which produces our
color caste system is dynamic; it is concerned to maintain
even at the point of violence the power of the white race over
all comers. And all of these centers of strife seek aggressively
for the support of public opinion without which they cannot
hope to succeed. The constant competition for the backing of
the public is an expression of the basic rivalries for power
around which society turns.[20]

It is the fact of power that gives groups their significance.
Whether these be well-knit organizations, or general expressions of group consciousness, they are important for society
because of their power. From the moral point of view, this
power and these organizations are neutral in themselves. They
are neither good nor bad; their value or their evil depends
entirely upon the use which is made of them. This moral
neutrality, however, must not be allowed to blind us to their
crucial importance. Groups and the power which gives
them significance are one of the most basic features of our
culture.

(3) *The substitution of a mechanical for a spiritual unity.*
The third main characteristic of our society is the substitution
of a mechanical unity for a spiritual one. This has not been a
sudden transition; on the contrary, the spiritual disintegration
with which we are faced has been in process for centuries, as has
been the development of mechanical unity. The vividness with
which we may discern the change is due to the fact that, so far

[20] *Ibid.*, pp. 61-68.

as can be observed, we are virtually at the end of the process. Although there has never been unity among all the peoples of the world, the spiritual unity which once characterized the dominant Western peoples has disappeared, and has been replaced by an intricate network of ties which are the result of the machine.

Though it is easy to idealize a past age, there can be little doubt that medieval civilization was held together by a unity which was in essence spiritual. Amos Wilder has well said:

> The sum total of evil has probably not changed greatly, for the Middle Ages had their own way of brutalizing men and sabotaging the weal of successive generations, of condemning men and women before birth to attentuated and warped and blasted lives.[21]

Yet that there was an overarching loyalty, and that this loyalty was of a high spiritual nature, cannot be denied. The influence of the Church was pervasive, and although the age did not approach the achievement of the Christian ethic, in its main cultural expressions and in much of its life, Christianity was the conscious goal of endeavor.

It is, accordingly, from the end of the medieval period that the breakdown of this unity may be dated.

> The new or renewed knowledge, the new and powerful social forms, the explorations, brought about a growing revolt against the static patterns of life and thought that had so long given a degree of unity and order to the West.[22]

The Renaissance and the Enlightenment, the one standing for a new freedom in thought and the other for a new reliance upon human wisdom, and both for a new individualism, worked a

[21] Amos N. Wilder, Vol. I, p. 137.
[22] *Ibid.*, pp. 138-39.

double corrosive upon the old standards. A compact, definite, stable world became virtually infinite; the cosmos was apparently unlimited, and the reaches of the human mind seemed indefinite. The prominence of human reason, and the faith men put in it, made faithful dependence upon God unnecessary; secularism began its rise. This was validated by the achievements of science, both theoretical and practical. Discoveries, the growth of cities, the accumulation of national power made it seem as though man could manage his own affairs. A movement of revolution, idealism and emotional release, known as Romanticism, further accentuated the basic humanism already current. The individual began to assume more and more importance in the eyes of men, and the necessity of community and cultural unity, less. Here was in process a cultural breakdown, accomplished not only through the sterility of the old, but also through the vigor of the new.

This vigor, however, had not sufficient strength to establish a new synthesis. The clash of peoples in two wars that could not be isolated but which spread throughout the world burns into our minds the fact that we have no unity among us strong enough to keep the nations from one another's throats. We have rather a series of expressions of cultural anarchy. We may be in the habit of conforming to a number of social conventions, and law commands in some of us the respect which is due it, but fundamentally we are caught in an "anarchy of values," in a "loss of ritual" and in a pervasive "rootlessness" which give no common ground for the fundamental human urges out of which a cohesive culture is built.[23] There are, to be sure, values to which we hold, but these are isolated, frequently in conflict with one another, and do not stem from a single Value. We have valued science, given our loyalty to

[23] *Ibid.*, pp. 145-155.

democracy and raised the individual and humanity to a high pedestal in our scheme of things. Yet we have used science for the destruction of humanity, and our valuation of humanity has not been strong enough to force us to extend democracy to the most vital areas of life. It is not that we do not believe; the trouble is that our faiths, lacking a single focus in the Eternal, are contradictory and shallow. This is dramatized in our contemporary loss of ritual. There are holidays enough, but except for the automobile trip, attendance at the movies and the shooting of firecrackers we do not know how to observe them. Although speeches on the significance of Independence Day, Labor Day and Memorial Day are multitudinous, and although on Christmas and Easter we go to church in vast numbers, these days have but little basic significance for our individual living and almost none as expressions of the convictions of our society. There is here a dry formalism, defined largely by the action of the government and industry, underneath which is only the anarchy of individually formed opinion.

At least one comprehensive cause for this condition is the rootlessness of our living, an isolation of existence which in turn had its rise in the breakdown of the medieval unity. The progress of science depends upon the spirit of free inquiry and of questioning. Upon this spirit rest the stupendous achievements of the modern age; yet this has become hardened into a philosophy which makes of this spirit of inquiry an absolute faith by which we must live. "Scientism" has as its characteristic mood a fundamental skepticism and distrust of traditional values.[24] The scientific age, therefore, is one that is not conscious of its spiritual and intellectual forebears; it has cut its roots from the past and seeks to live under the guidance

[24] For a discussion of scientism, see Elton Trueblood, Vol. II, pp. 37-38, and Frederick West, Volume II, pp. 158-67.

only of its own insights. Sociological developments, moreover, have added to rootlessness in a different fashion. Concentration of population in the cities, and the general prestige which is attendant upon city life, have tended to dissociate men from nature; life is lived in areas where the great natural rhythms are little in evidence. Men are ignorant of their dependence upon nature, and the grandeur of nature has no opportunity to humble and refresh their souls. Nor has urban culture provided a more intense sense of community. The opposite has occurred, social anonymity and personal individualism being the general atmosphere within which the city dweller moves. The mood has been well caught by T. S. Eliot:

> Here is a place of disaffection
> Time before and time after
> In a dim light—
>   Only a flicker
> Over the strained time-ridden faces
> Distracted from distraction by distraction
> Filled with fancies and empty of meaning
> Tumid apathy with no concentration
> Men and bits of paper, whirled by the cold wind
> That blows before and after time,
> Wind in and out of unwholesome lungs.[25]

Most important, however, is our loss of cosmic ties. Our society does not live in devotion to God. The Church has been forced into retreat, and no longer holds sway over those impersonal relations of our common life which are of such increasing importance. Its voice once heard with effectiveness

[25] "Burnt Norton," from *Four Quartets* (New York: Harcourt, Brace and Company, Inc., 1943). Quoted by permission. See Amos N. Wilder, Vol. I, p. 149.

in the spheres of international relations and politics and of economic life is now the voice of a small minority, and the powers go their way for the most part unaffected. Even in the realm of personal relationships, the Church is on the defensive; there is not that common acceptance of its basic faith which gives ethical judgment its enabling power.[26] This is seen clearly also in the extent of mental illness which characterizes our time. Though we shall return to this presently, it must be noted that the frustrations and aggressions of our troubled spirits stem in essence from a failure to "look God in the eye." The healing of repentance and humility and acknowledgment of guilt before God is rarely achieved.[27] Our age has lost its roots of faith, and therein is the crux of its spiritual disunity.

Our society, however, does have its unity. It is the unity of interconnection, in essence mechanical. Though we are not bound together by the ties of common loyalty and observance and ethics, we are close knit in the functions of life. Here we see clearly the extent of the substitution which has been made: the long process of breakdown has carried with it a correlative process of construction. But they have been on different levels: the unity which was spiritual has been replaced not by a counterpart but by an opposite.

The mechanical unity of our time has two forms: the interdependence of the parts of our society and the communication which is possible between them. We need spend little time in describing the degree to which we are dependent upon our distant neighbors and they on us. The discovered bankruptcy of a few financial concerns in New York was sufficient to light

[26] For a discussion of this retreat, see James H. Nichols, Vol. I, pp. 171-87.
[27] Walter M. Horton, Vol. I, pp. 133-34.

the dry rot of the economic structure of the late twenties, causing economic misery to spread throughout the world. A recent strike of the soft coal miners forthwith stopped the production of steel, upon which every heavy industry and most light industries depend. The decision of longshoreman in New York to stop work meant that the hunger of persons in the heart of Europe was unrelieved. A pistol shot in Sarajevo and an incident on a bridge at Marco Polo were so bound up with other events that the lives of millions were placed in jeopardy. The discovery of a scientific formula in the quiet study of an exiled Jew has cast an utterly different complexion upon the entire political structure of the world. There is little point in multiplying examples; the fact of importance is that this unity is in essence mechanical. That is, it is a unity of interdependent parts, any one of which being affected has its result, beneficial or disastrous, upon the whole.

The unity which is achieved through communication is likewise obvious. It is equally mechanical. Culture does not fly the skyways nor does it roll upon the freight cars. Though news is available to us instantaneously from all parts of the world, and though we may within a few hours visit any land that strikes our fancy, this is evidence more of the perfection of machines than of the emergence of a common culture. The significance of the speed and ease of communication is found in the degree to which it enhances the interdependence of which we have been speaking. The transportation of goods means the opening of markets and the dependence of economies upon them. The communication of news, particularly of important political and economic events, has a vital influence upon the conduct of these affairs within each nation of the earth. In interdependence and communication we have the main features of our contemporary mechanical unity, and in the substitution of this for the spiritual unity which underlay other ages, we have the most telling clew as to the nature of our own.

(4) *Personal tensions leading toward disastrous rather than creative life.* The fourth characteristic of our society concerns its effect upon basic personal tensions. The individual is never free from tensions; they are part of life itself.[28] Birth, growth, vocation, marriage, personal and social changes and death all produce their attractions and repulsions for the individual mind and spirit. In all ages and throughout all of life there is the possibility of both conflict and reconciliation between the person and himself, his environment and his Creator.[29] This is normal and inescapable. That which is distinctive in any society, however, is the tendency of these tensions to be destructive or creative. It is the degree to which they are destructive in our time that is important.

Evidence is found in the types and general causes of personal tensions in society. Psychoses and neuroses are typical, and though great strides have been made in their treatment "modern civilization seems to produce neurotics and psychotics faster than psychiatrists can treat them."[30] For these, however, there is a general background:

> Unhappiness, frustration and mental confusion are so widespread in the modern world that they constitute a kind of chronic, collective ailment, which makes people susceptible to acute mental breakdowns from time to time, much as a severe cold may make them susceptible to an attack of pneumonia.[31]

[28] *Ibid.,* p. 110.
[29] *Ibid.,* p. 108.
[30] *Ibid.,* pp. 110-11.
[31] *Ibid.,* p. 111.

Here is the drift of mental tension in our time: from the atmosphere of general discontent to the more acute forms of mental illness. Pre-neurotic unhappiness shows up in more severe psychoneuroses in which the emotional life of a person is badgered by ungrounded feelings of inferiority and fears and obsessions as well as by a continuing fatigue. Or it may issue in hysteria, with its crippling physical effect. These, however, are the less serious neuroses; the line runs to even more drastic disorders, the utter deadness of the schizophrenic, the distorted and frequently violent reaction of the paranoid, and the alternating brightness and darkness which besets the manic-depressive.[32]

The causes of these difficulties are complex, and the subject of ceaseless psychological research. For the most part, they are outside the bounds of our discussion, except for two major points. There is general agreement that they are to be found in the impact of the contradictions and the tensions of the social environment upon the individual, an impact which has its most telling effect in early childhood. The influence of the family group is itself profound and, to a greater degree than the layman suspects, determinative. The influence of brother and sister and mother and father upon the sensitivities of the developing child has the effect of permanently molding his personality. But homes, as well as the other influences which play upon the child, are to a large extent the transmitters of the tensions of the culture and society of which they are a part. Psychological tension cannot be understood apart from an understanding of the basic evils in the surrounding culture.[33]

We have already hinted, however, at the fundamental prob-

[32] See *Ibid*, pp. 108-14, for a fuller discussion of all of these types of mental illness.

[33] See further *Ibid.*, pp. 114-25.

lem. The ancient tensions between a man and himself, his environment and his Creator cannot be resolved creatively in a social milieu which does not possess a unifying faith. A mechanical unity hardly provides the center around which the variations and depths of human personality may be integrated. Without faith in God, both individual and society will never fail to show the symptoms of mental disease.

> When God and conscience are repressed, only nature and mankind remain upon the scene; and throughout the history of the modern age they have fought an endless, inconclusive duel. When nature's end of the seesaw is up and man seems to be nature's victim, man succumbs to romantic melancholy and despair. When man's end is up, and he thinks for a moment to have become literally the master of nature, he becomes as elated as a maniac— until the next blow falls, and humiliates him again. Advances in scientific knowledge can never cure these recurrent humiliations; we know that finally, now that atomic power is in our hands. The only cure for humiliation and frustration is humility and repentance—acknowledgement of guilt in the sight of God.[34]

We need not repeat that this is the crucial factor which we lack. Here is the clew to the fact that the contemporary tensions in personal living are not creative, but are destructive of the unlimited possibilities of the human personality.

2. THE CHALLENGE TO CHRISTIANITY

It remains to indicate how each of the four main characteristics of our age which we have described constitutes a challenge to Christianity. It is obvious that there are undesirable and positively evil elements in each; it is also true that

[34] *Ibid.,* pp. 133-34.

in each, except perhaps the last, there are elements of good. What then is the challenge?

(1) *In different ways, each of the above four characteristics leads to a denial of man's full stature.* Our common obsession with economic activity indicates at root a truncated interest. Here, as in the case of any passion, men's energies are all directed in one channel. Our object in life is to acquire the ease and the comfort and the power which economic goods, or their symbol, money, will provide. This is an all-consuming object. It is, as we noted, necessary; but it is inadequate. Economic activity is not fully expressive of man's capacities; his range of interests is wider, infinitely wider, than even the complex and varied range of work which contemporary economic structure calls forth. For instance, men have been largely cut off from the interests which develop and support "higher culture." The concerns of the intellect, except for those in the universities, are largely denied; or if they are not denied they are made subservient to the practical use to which they may be put. Even in the universities the dominance of pragmatism and vocationalism is marked.[35] Contemporary achievements worthy to be ranked with the classics in literature, art, music and philosophy are notably absent. Such interests as do persist outside the realm of economic life tend to be warped. The interest in family life, fundamental to the health of all cultures, is rarely in ours an interest which lives in itself. The success of family life is measured by its comfort; the motive for striving is frequently saving so that another mechanical item may be purchased. Family schedules revolve, necessarily, around the hours—which may be any of the day or night—of the bread-winner: the whole family becomes molded by the demands of father's job. Here is an interest which persists, but which has

[35] See further Frederick West, Vol. II, pp. 167-74.

become warped, even as other concerns have been virtually eliminated. Our obsession with economic life has foreshortened the range of human interests.

Fundamental human freedom, by which is meant the ability of persons to develop fully as persons, is also limited. The dominance of groups and the rivalry for power in which they inevitably engage have the total effect of eliminating vast potentialities of human growth. The centralization of economic power, for instance, means that control of the livelihood, the homes, the avocations, the leisure of countless numbers of persons resides in the hands of a few. Those who are on top may or may not cherish their power and responsibility; they may or may not use it wisely. The fact remains that in the decisions which they make, in the efficiency with which they run their immense concerns there rests the fate of nations. The same is true, as all the world has learned to its grief, of the concentration of national power. Wars which sweep the entire populace are contingent upon the use of this power. No one can view either actually or in imagination the desperate plight of the displaced persons in Europe and the refugees in Asia without realizing the extent to which human freedom is limited by the power which organized nationalities have over the race. Nor can one see the fear in the eyes of the Negro who must in every move safeguard the myth of white supremacy lest he lose his life, and come away feeling that he has been in the presence of a free man. In some organizations, as in those avowedly or implicitly fascist groups which seek power in American life,[36] and as in the mass mind of the white man, the limitation of freedom is designed and sinister. In other groupings, it is the result of the historical process through which we are going, and victimizes both those who are on top and those who are

[36] Howard Thurman, Vol. II, pp. 82-99.

on the bottom. However responsibility may ultimately be assigned, the dominance of groups, both organized and unorganized, is the chief source of the limitation of human freedom in the contemporary scene.

In the development which has resulted in the substitution of a mechanical for a spiritual unity, there is implicit a denial of the range of man's responsiveness. The culture of the ages and of the civilizations is eloquent testimony to the degree to which men are responsive to beauty, to nature, to ideas. Given a conducive spiritual climate, man finds in this responsiveness his highest creativity. Yet the dominant atmosphere of our culture is cold, mechanical and limited, containing no provision for that self-transcendence from which the products of reflection and artistic application spring. It is a busy society, and its business is with things. The mechanical beat of jazz music and the straight lines of modernistic art indicate our subservience to the materialism of the time. We are barred from nature; we have no time for philosophy save that which will insure the getting of more things; our attention to music is usually a better form of escape from the hurry of the day. We are not provided, in our mechanistic time, with the spiritual unity which alone can release creative cultural effort. Our range of responsiveness is cut down.

This might conceivably be overcome, were the personal tensions under which we live productive of creative life. But their sum total is destructive. The general background of unhappiness yields such acute and varied forms of mental illness that the flowering of human personality is achieved only rarely and upon the exercise of severe discipline. Energies are, in other words, dissipated; that which might be creative is, largely through no individual fault, destructive. Although it is dangerous to dissociate responsibility among the generations for general social evil, it may nevertheless be said that the child of the modern home enters an atmosphere of such difficult tension, that he stands only a slight chance of so developing as to use the total energy with which he is endowed. Human power is, so to speak, nipped in the bud; there is immense wastage, not only in the fact of underdevelopment through destructive tensions, but also in the fact of outright decay.

A truncated human interest; loss of basic freedom; the denial of the range of human responsiveness; the dissipation of energies. It is these with which Christianity is faced. What is the common core? It is that those influences which are uppermost in contemporary society conspire to produce the depersonalization of men. They work in different ways, each limiting or perverting or wasting the human spirits and minds and bodies of which civilization is built. Seen from the viewpoint of the individual, they rob him of his humanity. Because they are in operation, he is less of a man than he might otherwise be. Potentially he has a wide range of interests, he has freedom to develop, he has responses which issue in the highest form of creativity, he has energies unbounded with which to carry on his life to the full. These are denied. He is depersonalized. Seen from the viewpoint of society as a whole, this means that it is the impersonal forces which are dominant. Things, power, mechanical relations: these are the factors with which life today is concerned, and with drastic personal results. Depersonalization is the central challenge of the time.

(2) *The aim of Christianity.* It is the claim of Christianity that man is made in the image of God; he is a reflection of the nature of his Creator. God is not an impersonal force; on the contrary, the means which He has chosen to reveal His character show that He is in the deepest sense personal. God has not revealed Himself primarily through a philosophical

system, nor through the establishment of a model social order. God has revealed Himself in a man. Here is the clearest indication that the Being of God, whatever else it may contain, is possessed of the depth and vibrancy and creative expression which have their lesser counterparts in the human spirit.

It is also the claim of Christianity that the image of God in man has been dulled, almost lost. This is the meaning of the story of the Fall; here it is set forth that man by some means has become less than he was created to be, that a crust now hides his true nature. The explanation of Christian theology is that this crust consists of proud ambition: the refusal to recognize that God is God, and the desire to put the human self in the center of the universe. Modern psychological and ethical theory speak of this as the ego which, in its overweening anxiety to be all things to the individual, pushes his true responsiveness to God and his fellows into the far reaches of the subconscious mind. Here is the wall between man and God, a wall which defaces the original image.

The aim of Christianity is the restoration of the image. It is a third part of the Christian claim that man may be brought again to his full stature. As there is in force at present an alienation from the Creator, so there may be a reconciliation to Him. "God was in Christ reconciling the world unto himself." In Christ is the full stature of manhood, reconciled to God. This is the possibility which the revelation of God in Christ holds open to all men. The claim of the Christian faith is that the egocentric crust which now holds down and stifles the full range of capacities in the human soul may be dissipated, to the end that man in all of his potentialities may again exhibit the image of God.

(3) *The vital conflict.* It is clear that there is a vital conflict between such a claim and the character of the modern world.

The depersonalization of men which contemporary society accomplishes cuts across the very nerve center of the Christian faith. The two are utterly opposed. The result of the one is to make of man less than he already is. Not only is there little help for his egocentricity in contemporary society; the major forces of it conspire to rob him of the potentialities he possesses for overcoming this egocentricity. On the other hand, Christianity claims not only that man is less than he might be, but offers the power and the resolution of the guilt which are necessary to restore him to his true stature.

This is the essence of the challenge. It is a challenge which contains breadth and depth and height. Its breadth is that of society, for it is idle to suppose any widespread recovery short of thorough readjustment in the social structure itself. The fact that the individual is so largely in the impersonal hands of social forces is the key to the need for reorganization in the interests of justice. The depth of the challenge is the depth of human personality. Reorganization alone will not do. There must be a fundamental reorientation of the human spirit, by which its latent power and its creative responses may be brought forth and directed to God and to the interests of mankind. And the height of the challenge is that of an overarching cultural unity. Reorganized structures and changed humans need an energizing center. Culture itself, by which society lives and breathes, must be directed so that it will contribute to the increased stature of man. This means that God must be the center of its loyalty, and the motive of its responses. The restoration in man of the image of God, in the face of a social order which contributes mainly to his further depersonalization, is the challenge which Christianity faces.

2

THE FUNCTION OF THE CHURCH

*1. The unique possession of the Church is a Gospel. 2. The
function of the Church in establishing the Gospel in the lives of
people. 3. Social transformation as a derivitive function.
4. The universal responsibility of the Church. 5. The Church
as the soul of the world: Christendom, world community, the
Gospel as judge, guide and power.*

WE cannot well understand how the challenge of our age
may be met without a view of the basic function of the Church.
Christian loyalty is not one which can be bent this way and
that, with the varying winds of culture. True, there must always
be an adjustment of approach and method; Christians must
"be all things to all men," but their fundamental allegiance
is constant. So also is the underlying character of the community or fellowship into which Christians are drawn. By the
"Church" we mean here, of course, not primarily ecclesiastical
institutions or the sum total of them. These are the "churches,"
brought into existence by a more fundamental reality which
is the spiritual bond formed among all who have faith in
Christ, namely, the universal fellowship of the Church. This
fellowship has a distinctive function, which may be understood
in terms of the following four propositions:

(1) *The unique possession of the Church is a Gospel.* This

28

Gospel is not a social program, nor a metaphysical system, nor a psychology. Nor is its chief burden the works of an institution or a series of them. All of these to be sure are involved in the Gospel. From it have come great schemes for social organization, systems of philosophy, and clews to psychological understanding. It has given rise to the oldest and most far-reaching single institution on the face of the earth. Yet this Gospel cannot be equated with any of these; it has its own character. The Gospel is a proclamation about the relationship between God and man.

The Gospel is a proclamation that in Jesus Christ man is reconciled to God. We spoke at the close of the last chapter of the claim of Christianity that it can restore the original image of God in man; that the wall which now separates men from God, causing them to wander and to lead their fellows into the blind alleys of life, may be broken down, with the result that the true way may be made apparent. The center of the Christian claim is that this is accomplished in Jesus Christ. As John Knox has so well pointed out,[1] there is involved in this center, which we call Jesus Christ, an absolutely decisive event for the human race. The faith of Christians in Jesus Christ is not simply a faith in a good man, the mere record of whose life still stirs the hearts of people; nor is it a faith in any single aspect of that life. Even the death of Jesus and his resurrection cannot be considered singly. There is here a series of happenings in which there is a unifying tie of such distinctive and crucial import that we may speak of the whole only as an Event. This unity, which gives not only cohesiveness, but imparts *decisive* character to the whole, is nothing less than the fact that Almighty God has in this event broken into the life

[1] Vol. III, chap. 1.

of the human race, and there in the form of a human being has disclosed His nature and accomplished His purposes for us.

There is more here than disclosure, infinitely more than information, however broadly these terms may be taken. There is here the fact that the God of the heavens and the earth has chosen as the primary means of His action among us a human person. He has singled out one of *us*; one in whose heart there rose hopes and in whose spirit desires had their play, even as in ours. He has taken a man, subject to the suffering we are subject to, as well as to the fears and the courage to overcome them. In such a man, God caused His will to be done. Each of us can only stand in reverence before the fierceness of Jesus' desert struggle and at the edge of the turmoil in the garden. But whatever else our reverence may teach us, we know that here was one in whom the will of the Father was perfectly accomplished. This is to say that in Jesus Christ man has been reconciled to God. The impossible task of overcoming the sinfulness of man by the goodness of God has actually been accomplished in Jesus Christ. He is one of us and therefore our representative; all that is human has been gathered up in him and transformed; the wall between mankind and its Creator has been breached. This is not, however, simply an action which is past and to which we may assent or with which we may disagree. It is an event which contains a continuing power. From Jesus Christ there has burst new life, which nineteen hundred years later has produced martyrdoms matching in their courage those of the early years of the Christian movement. We do not deal with a dead fact; we deal with an event which, then and now, awakens a moving response in men. This is the response of faith, that response which, transcending the range and influence of human reason, is able to turn men around, so that thoughts and acts, minds and will, have a new center, which is God. Thus the reconciliation of man to God not only has taken place, it still is taking place. This is that aspect of the Gospel which declares that God loves the world.

The Gospel is the proclamation that there is on earth a new community of men who are bound together by discipleship to Christ. The Church is the evidence of the fact that the life of Jesus Christ is neither an isolated nor a dead event. For the Church is the continuation, in the lives of other men, of the distinctive spirit which gave to Jesus his decisive character. The Church is the Body of Christ. It is the community of them that are reconciled to the Father and in whom there has been awakened the response of faith which has made that reconciliation possible. This does not mean that our churches are composed of perfect people, nor that they are perfect themselves. The sinfulness and corruption of the churches are all too evident, and their limitations are apparent on every hand.[2] It does mean, however, that that force which the Church has called the Holy Spirit continues to move within the souls of men, causing them to repent and to turn their lives toward God. The response of the faithful to Christ is not in essence like a person's admiration for a beautiful painting; nor is the community of the faithful similar to the associations of those who are attracted by the work of a particular artist. The Church exists because the Spirit of Christ was not destroyed on the cross but lives; and men are in the Church not through their own decisions primarily but because this Spirit has sought them out and has caused a rebirth in their lives.

It is clear, therefore, that the Church is not formed by the consent of men. It is not an association; it is a new community which has been created by God. The beginnings of this new

[2] See further John C. Bennett, Vol. III, chap. 6.

creation are found in the Old Testament,[3] in the covenant of mutual responsibility which was instituted between God and the people of Israel. In this covenant there was reached an understanding whereby God would be the leader of Israel, and Israel would worship God alone. In essence this was not a mere mechanical agreement, but rather the response of a people to the bidding of a Being whom they ultimately recognized as the Creator of life. This covenant was renewed and transformed in the New Testament. The completeness of the revelation of God in Jesus Christ, and the power which that revelation contained in it, meant that henceforth the community was to have its center in him and in his living spirit. The way by which the original covenant was to be fulfilled by men, and the power with which it was to be carried out was now made clear and available to the human race. In both the covenant of Israel and the Church of the Christians, the primary force is not the will of men. God is the principal actor in this drama: the outlines of its theme and the means of its enactment are all from Him.

The distinctive characteristic of the Church is love. Not, obviously, a sentimental emotion; but the determination of will which makes it possible for one to bear a cross, and the subjugation of self which makes it possible for one to say, "It is not I who live, but Christ lives within me." "By this," Jesus said, "men shall know that you love me, if you love one another." If the Church is the community of those who are faithful and who are reconciled to God, the content and the test of this faith and this reconciliation are love. This is the Spirit which binds the new community. It is in the Church,

[3] See further James Muilenberg, "The Faith of Ancient Israel," in *The Vitality of the Christian Tradition*, George F. Thomas, ed. (New York: Harper & Brothers, 1944). Also, Paul Scherer, Vol. III, chap. 2.

therefore, that there is the first evidence that the world has begun to love God.

The Gospel is the proclamation that life on earth is not our total experience, but that eternal life is to come. Here again, the continuity of the whole is made evident. Jesus Christ and the Church cannot be considered as simply the means which Providence has used for the amelioration of life on earth. Granted that life would be utterly empty without the meaning and power which Christ and the Chruch hold for it, the underlying significance of the whole is on a still deeper level. It is found in the fact that a *qualitatively different* realm of existence, namely, the realm of eternal life, life, that is, not subject to the decay and ultimate death which characterize merely human existence, has been offered to men. The response in men's souls which is evoked by Jesus Christ is the initial entrance into this different realm; and it is the Gospel that no power can again separate us from it. This is the meaning of the victory over the grave; not that human death is abolished, but that it is not final. It is somewhat startling to find in the work of a modern historian such a sentence as the following:

> As we come to the effects of Christianity, we must again remind ourselves that what from the standpoint of Christian faith are the most important escape the historian's art. The Christian declares that only a small segment of his life is lived within history and that the most significant fruitage is in the infinitely longer period beyond the grave and time.[4]

The reconciliation and love made possible in the present life are but a foreshadowing of the full entrance into the realm of

[4] Kenneth Scott Latourette, *Advance Through Storm*, Vol. VII of "A History of the Expansion of Christianity" series (New York: Harper & Brothers, 1945) p. 489.

eternal life which is to come. In the faith that this is but a
transitory existence, that the limitations and ending of human
life are not final, but that there is a future of which this life is
a present foreshadowing, the Gospel reaches its climax.

In broadest outlines[5] this is the Gospel which is the unique
possession of the Church. However it may be stated and re-
stated, it is always in essence a gospel concerning the relationship between man and God. Whatever may be its implications,
and they are many, this is the center of its message. Both the
fact that the Gospel is the unique possession of the Church, and
the content of this Gospel, are of determinative significance for
the function of the Church in the world.

(2) *The basic function of the Church has been to establish
the Gospel in the lives of people.* From a recognition of the
primacy of the Gospel, we turn to the fact that in essence it is
the business of the Church to make this vital in the lives of
men. It is a point which at first sight may seem obvious and
hardly worth arguing. Yet on all hands, particularly in view
of the chaos of our world civilization and the fear which this
chaos brings forth among us all, the Church is called upon to
be the savior of our times. The appeal is just, and the responsibility of the Church is clear. Yet how may that responsibility
be fulfilled? How may the Church, if it is to be loyal to its
genius, proceed if it is to be the hope of mankind?

We need not engage on a long historical analysis to dis-
cover what the Church has considered to be its fundamental
function in the world. The clew is found decisively in the
reaction of the Church when it has been pressed by avowedly
non-Christian peoples. Here, if at any time, the Church may
be expected to perform those tasks which are most necessary

---

[5] For a more complete discussion of each of these three aspects of
the Gospel, see Vol. III, chap. 1-3.

and most in accord with its underlying character. We shall make brief reference to three periods of pressure from non-Christian peoples in the history of the Church: the beginning of the Church, the time of the fifth-century invasions of the Roman Empire from the north, and the era of the expansion of the European peoples. There are, of course, vast differences in the nature of these pressures, yet they have in common a challenge of such proportions as to constitute a threat to the Gospel itself.

The early Christians were set in the midst of a pagan, immoral and hostile world. Both official and popular religion were antithetical to the Christian faith: emperor worship, mystery religions and astrology presented absolute denials. The conceptions of philosophy, particularly neo-Platonism and Stoicism, though they offered valuable points of contact with Christianity, were in essence secular. And the popular preaching of Stoic morals which came into vogue shortly after the advent of Christianity did only a little to mitigate the licentiousness and the open cruelty which marked customary morality. Slavery was accepted; great divergences in wealth and poverty were the rule; family ties were unstable. To such an unfavorable religious and moral climate was added the fact of open hostility, both popular and official, resulting in petty persecutions and in concerted attempts to obliterate the followers of The Way.

By the fifth century, the picture had radically changed. Christianity had unseated the ancient gods, and had been for over a century established in the seat of power. It had to considerable degree corrected the flagrant moral abuses of the earlier time. Yet a deeper difficulty was at hand: the dissolution of the Roman Empire was proceeding apace. Added to internal decay, was the pressure from without. From the time of Marcus Aurelius, peoples from north had been pressing upon the outer borders of the Empire, and although they had been withstood successfully, their force by the fifth century could no longer be denied. Allamani, Franks, Visigoths, Ostrogoths, Burgundians, Lombards, Saxons, Huns, Alans, Suevi, Angles, Jutes—all during the fifth century invaded the Empire from Britain through Gaul to the heart of Rome. Here was a situation the Church had not faced before. Taking the period as a whole, from the time of the restrained pressure on the borders of the Empire through the period of the actual invasions, the Church was in the position of being closely allied with a decadent civilization, and at the same time faced with the vigor of a series of invading peoples. Here indeed was a curious reversal of the situation of the early days: then the threat had been from the general hostility of a pagan environment; now the threat was not only from the paganism of external forces, but also from the fact that the social and cultural milieu in which the Church had risen to power and which now supported it, was itself giving way to the vigor from without.

An even greater change was apparent when, beginning in the fifteenth century, the relatively settled culture of Europe began to expand. We have in mind at this point not so much the internal expansion which was marked by the Renaissance and later by the Protestant Reformation, but rather the move-ment of exploration, of emigration, of commercial develop-ment and of political domination which from the initial journey of Columbus proceeded apace through the nineteenth century. Here again the Church was put in the presence of multitudes of non-Christians, but in a manner which differed sharply from the situation in either the first or the fifth century. The Church was identified with a culture which it had been the primary factor in molding; it was not a tiny minority in an unfriendly

world. The culture with which it was connected was not threatened from without and decadent internally; on the contrary,
it was giving evidence, from the first dawning of the redis-
covered learning of the Renaissance through all of the complex
factors which gave rise to nation states and the industrial
revolution, of the most astounding vitality. It was not only
soundly based, but it was spilling over, extending its influences into the far corners of the globe. The forces which made
for this expansion were largely secular: science made travel
possible and relatively safe; the pressure of the economic needs
of an increasingly urban civilization in addition to the lure
of markets in themselves gave rise to an expanding·commerce;
and with the traders went the representatives of government.
With the important and intriguing question of the influence
of Christianity upon this entire movement, we cannot here be
concerned. Undoubtedly its influence was great. Yet the means
and the motive which were behind the expansion were not
religious and were not in their fundamental character representative of the Church. Obviously, however, as people from a
Christian culture traveled, settled, reported their findings, and
gained control over the peoples of other lands, the Church
came into complex contact with non-Christian peoples, complex
because it met, on the one hand, the tribal life of Africa and
the Islands, and, on the other hand, the ancient and subtle and
vast civilizations of the Orient. The immediate threat to the
Church was not so pronounced as in its encounter with Rome
and the invaders from northern Europe; yet over the long
range, this association of the Church with the peoples of the
world during the period of the expansion of Europe was one
of the most critical of its history.

The essential challenge to the Church differs as greatly in
each of the three periods as do the circumstances which pro-

duced it. In the first century it was a question of life or death. Would the seed which had been so inauspiciously sown in such an unhealthy soil grow at all, much less flower? Would the small band of poor and ignorant followers, who possessed no weapons of organization or power or prestige or wisdom of the world, succeed in the great commission which they understood was theirs? The impartial observer would have been forced to answer with a resounding "No." The odds were so heavily against them that the death of the small movement of The Way seemed only a matter of time. Here was the clear-cut issue of the few against the many. In the fifth century, however, the challenge was more complex. The association of the Church with the Empire, decaying at the roots and now well up into the branches, might well have meant that Church as well as Empire would go down before the advancing northern peoples. Granted that the Church shared the prestige which attached to the Empire, and that this prestige assisted its work with the invaders, would it not nevertheless decline with the decline of Rome? This was not the challenge of the many by the few; this was the challenge to generate a vitality which, standing firm amid a disintegrating culture, would be such as to win an alien and more vigorous people.

From the fifteenth to the nineteenth (and even twentieth) centuries, the issue was still different. The forces which were accomplishing the expanding influence of European culture and which were carrying the European peoples to the ends of the earth were secular. Would the Church be made the servant of science, commerce and nationalism? The need was for increased vitality, but of a different sort from that which would capture for Christ the invaders of the fifth century. The vitality which was needed was that which would overarch the dominantly imperialistic trends of the time, transcending them, in order that the impact of the Church upon the non-Christian peoples would be the impact of the Gospel. This also was a life-and-death issue, though not in the clear-cut terms of the first century. Presumably the Church could ride on secular currents for perhaps generations; to do so, however, would have spelled the ultimate extinction of the faith.

In each of these diverse situations, the basic response of the Church has been the same. It is important to repeat the fact that we are dealing with the basic response. Clearly, the different nature of the tasks presented by each situation has necessitated a widely varying range of work. Yet in its first and basic response, the Church has shown a steady consistency.

Little time need be spent upon the work of the first-century church; testimony from the book of Acts is clear:

> Truly I perceive that God shows no partiality, but in every nation any one who fears him and does what is right is acceptable to him. You know the word which he sent to Israel, preaching good news of peace by Jesus Christ (he is Lord of all), the word which was proclaimed throughout all Judea, beginning from Galilee after the baptism which John preached: how God anointed Jesus of Nazareth with the Holy Spirit and with power; how he went about doing good and healing all that were oppressed by the devil, for God was with him. And we are witnesses to all that he did both in the country of the Jews and in Jerusalem. They put him to death by hanging him on a tree; but God raised him on the third day and made him manifest, not to all the people but to us who were chosen by God as witnesses, who ate and drank with him after he rose from the dead. And he commanded us to preach to the people, and to testify that he is the one ordained by God to be judge of the living and the dead [Acts 10:34-42].[6]

[6] From the Revised Standard Version of the New Testament (copyright, 1946, by the International Council of Religious Education) and used by permission. The Biblical quotations in this volume are from this version.

This was their gospel and this was their task. "To preach . . . and to testify," the content of the preaching and of the testimony being an evangel with the power to change lives. In due time, of course, the simplicity of the witness was changed: attacks on the Christians made reasoned apologies necessary; as the original fire of conviction died out and Christian life settled into the observance of the new law, problems of discipline and of organization were added. Moreover, the repeated persecutions further complicated church life in that they produced those who, under pressure, denied their faith, and presented the Church with the problem of their discipline and re-entry into the fold. The inroads of heresy, particularly that of Gnosticism, made it imperative to define the faith of the Church in order that its truth might be preserved without distortion. It did not take long for the original evangel to gather about it complicating factors. Yet amid these growing activities and developments, the basic function remained the same. The evangelism of the early Christians had become normative: the function of the Church was to implant the Gospel in the lives of men. It is around this function that the development of apology, creeds, organization and discipline turned, for all of these were made necessary in order that the evangelistic task of the Church, which was on every hand recognized as its primary task, could proceed unimpeded.

The response to the northern invasions was equally clear cut. We unfortunately do not have full records of the work of the Church among those people, but there is one figure and one fact which is determinative. During the early encroachments of the northerners, the Visigoths had established a settlement north of the Danube. Intercourse between them and the Romans was frequent. Christianity was undoubtedly known among them at an early date, but the first concerted effort

among them was made during the fourth century by Ulfilas.
Records of his work, and that of his associates, do not persist,
largely owing to the fact that he was of the Arian conviction,
ruled heretical by the church of Rome. Nevertheless, we know
that it is to him, and to his translation of the Scriptures into
the Gothic tongue, that the conversion of the Goths is due.
Christianity rapidly spread among them, and likewise among
their neighbors. Ulfilas is typical of the response of the Church
to the advance of the northern invasions. His work led in part
to, and is representative of, an important further fact. This is
that not only the Visigoths, but the Ostrogoths, the Vandals in
part, the Burgundians and the Lombards, had all embraced the
Arian form of Christianity.

> It was of the utmost significance that when the walls
> of the empire were broken the Germans came, for the
> most part, not as enemies of Christianity. Had the
> Western empire fallen, as well it might, a century before,
> the story of Christianity might have been vastly different.[7]

Here is evidence of the fact that while the northern peoples
were still without the borders of the Empire, the response of
the Church had begun. It is evidence, as is the work of Ulfilas,
that the basic function of the Church in relation to non-
Christians remained the same as in the earliest day. It continued to be essentially evangelistic.

This function not only continued, but in the later period became ultimately so dominant as in a marked degree to be the
distinctive achievement of the Church for that period. Just as
the expansion of the European peoples is one of the great
epochs in the history of the race, so the missionary effort of
the Church, which culminated in the nineteenth century,

[7] Williston Walker, *A History of the Christian Church* (New York:
Charles Scribner's Sons, 1940), p. 130.

marked one of the chief eras in its life. The broad outlines of
the story are too well known and have been too well docu-
mented[8] to warrant repetition here. It is enough to note that
hardly a church in Christendom did not in its own way participate in this effort; that literally thousands of some of the
most able Christians of the West gave their lives in it; and that
the whole was initiated and supported by a vision of the universal character of the Christian revelation and by a consecra-
tion to it that has not had a parallel in Christian history. The
relationship between this effort of the Western churches and
the general outreach of Western culture, particularly in its
commercial and political aspects, is unquestionably close. That
the missionary work of the Church, however, was not absolutely dependent upon these secular forces is proved by its
results. With due allowance for individual exceptions, it is
true that the missionaries and their followers in the various
lands were not by and large the tools of imperialism, whether
cultural, economic or political. They were carriers of the
Gospel, for which claims conclusive evidence is found in the
existence today of native churches throughout the world, which
are among the most vigorous critics of the general imperialism
of the earlier day and the present. Here is again evident the
basic function of the Church. Although the activities of missions were and are varied, their central purpose and main
achievement have been the establishment of the Gospel in the
lives of the different peoples.

We need only recognize the fact that in each period—as
indeed throughout the life of the Church—the evangelistic
task and the environment have been closely associated. Even

[8] Kenneth Scott Latourette, "A History of the Expansion of Christianity," Series, Vols. III, IV, V, VI (New York: Harper & Brothers,
1939-44).

for the earliest Christians, the political unity of the Empire, its system of communications, and its growing cultural uniformity were assets upon which the evangelists could and did build, even as the more unfavorable elements in the society were challenges to their efforts. In the fifth century, the prestige resulting to the Church from its association with Rome was an asset, and doubtless used to the full. In part this was offset by the decay of Roman civilization, but, again, this decay made it necessary for the Church to assert itself with increased vigor as it met the invading peoples. Commerce, the protection of government, and the immense prestige of industrial society were an undoubted asset in the later period, as they were also an unquestioned danger, since to many they seemed to be the real reason behind the expansion of Christianity. However complex the relationship between society and the Church in its missionary work has been—and it has been very complex and profound, with results both good and evil— it has nevertheless not been determinative. The Church has carried on the evangelization of non-Christian peoples, both because of and in spite of its surrounding culture. In each case this has been the first and basic response of the Church to the presence of the non-Christian. In its central purpose, the Church has not aimed to impart native culture to those outside its boundaries, nor has it intended primarily to change the culture and social structure of those to whom it has taken the Gospel. Its fundamental attention has been directed toward the relationship between God and man.

(3) *A result, but only a result, of this basic function of evangelism has been the transformation of society*. To insist upon the primary character of the evangelistic work of the Church is not to neglect either the social implications of the Gospel or the social effectiveness which the Church has shown.

On the contrary, it is to place the work of social and cultural transformation in its proper perspective. Though it is a common lament that the Church has never been sufficiently thorough in its social reforms, that it has never "put the Gospel into practice," this is not wholly justified. The Church has profoundly altered its surrounding environment in each of its successive ages. The issue with which we are primarily concerned, however, is the fact that this work of civilization-building is an outgrowth of the more essential and underlying work of evangelism. As illustrations of the way in which this has been carried out, we may look briefly at three notable social achievements of different times in the history of the Church: the contribution of monasticism to the higher culture of Europe; the effect of the Wesleyan revival upon the social evils in British life of the time; and the influence of Protestantism upon the development of democracy.

In a real sense it is to the monastic movement that the higher culture of Europe until the beginning of the modern era (and in some indirect respects through the modern era) owes its greatest debt. From the time of Jerome in the fourth century to the full development of Scholasticism in the thirteenth, study was a central part of the work carried on in the monasteries and the mendicant orders. It was here that learning and research were seriously initiated in the early centuries and preserved during the dark ages and extended throughout Europe during the high Middle Ages. The monastic schools were the centers of European education. They provided instruction not only in religious subjects, but in literature, in the classical languages, history, philosophy, music, painting, sculpture and architecture, as well as in other subjects. The traditional equipment of the monastery was a library, a staff of copyists and a school. Here the Scriptures were reproduced without ceasing; here what is left to us of classical literature was preserved and copied; here the influences of learning, both liberal arts and fine arts, were spread through the thousands of students who attended classes. The schools and the teachers who were developed in them gave rise to the universities, which henceforth were to be the centers of learning in Europe. From the monasteries, moreover, and from the mendicant monastic orders came Thomas Aquinas and the Schoolmen, those who were to give final expression to the culture which had been for centuries generating throughout the realm. It was even, iron-ically, the monasteries which, through their preservation of the literature of antiquity and through the development of interest generally in the higher culture, provided the material and the fundamental background out of which the intellectual awak-ening of the Renaissance was born. Clearly, higher culture in Europe owed its existence and character to no single move-ment so much as it did to monasticism.

What was this movement which produced such telling re-sults? It was not either in its origin or continuing character designed as an educational enterprise of the Church. It was essentially a reassertion of the Gospel, called forth by cor-ruption in the Church, in the surrounding society or both. As such it was an effort to recapture the purity of the Christian life, in terms which seemed obvious to those of the period. The first of the monks, at the end of the third century, left the cities and their churches, and went into the desert to live in solitude, in order to protest primarily against the worldliness of the churches. The chaos of the fifth century invasions drove thousands into the monasteries which by that time had been formed, for it was only here that a Christian life seemed to them possible. By this time the worth of the monastic life had become sufficiently established to be a secure and permanent part of the life of the Church. The forms of monasticism were, of course, varied. Some monks were hermits, particularly in the early stages of the development; soon, however, the necessity—both for purposes of discipline and of life—of communities was apparent, and the monasteries began their rise. Still a third form, sometimes associated with monasteries and sometimes existing independently, was that which demanded the monastic way of life, but in service in and to the world. The great numbers of missionaries, to whom the conversion of Europe is largely due, and the Franciscans are notable examples. Throughout, however, there is a recognizable identity of life and purpose. Behind the three vows of chastity, poverty and obedience there was the intense desire—a desire of sufficient power to command the allegiance of thousands of men and women—to establish the Gospel in their own lives and in the lives of others. While it is tempting for the modern Protestant to criticize this conception of the Gospel with severity, the integrity of the intention must be recognized. Here was a sustained effort to achieve that relationship between God and man which was conceived to be true to Jesus. Further uniformity was given to the movement by the Rule of Benedict, a code of conduct for monks and for monasteries, at once sufficiently rigorous and flexible to be the guide of the monastic movement for centuries. It is important not only for the cohesiveness it gave to the whole, but particularly for the provision it contained for work. Indeed, so important did work become for the monastic vocation that it virtually assumed the place of a fourth vow. Four to five hours each day were set aside for it, and from these disciplined and regular activities of the monks came those cultural contributions for which the movement is so noted. It is, however, the relationship of work to the other vows that is important for us to note. It was a part of service, which in turn was part of the spiritual obedience which formed a main aspect of the monastic vow. The immense labors of the monasteries, in other words, were the results of the distinctive conception of the Gospel which they held.

The second illustration of social effectiveness to which we have reference is the contribution of the Wesleyan revival to reform in Britain. On almost every hand, life in eighteenth-century England presented challenges to Christianity. In both the Established and nonconforming churches, spiritual life was at a low ebb. Political appointment of the clergy and an open habit of ecclesiastical patronage, sinecures and pluralities hung like millstones around the neck of the National Church, depriving it of leadership and adding burdens of corruption. The utter rationalism of the fashionable Deism had had its influence on Christianity, sermons, literature and customs alike showing bondage to its sterility. Nor was there any other source of moral vigor: corruption in general life ran the gamut from high politics, to economics, the penal code and prisons, the prevalence of drunkenness and licentiousness, the treatment of children and the perversion of sport into wanton cruelty.[9] It was an age of oppression, of poverty, of overt corruption, and particularly an age in which there seemed to be no compelling moral force. Yet it was a period in which common people longed for righteousness. Underneath the sterility in religion, there was a popular piety of integrity. And a desire for moral probity was unquestionably awakened in the hearts of many persons by the prevalence of open evil.

Within this general scene the Wesleyan revival had its rise. In essence, this was a revival of vital, personal religion: a revival which in the vigor of its commitment cut through the

[9] J. Wesley Bready, *England: Before and after Wesley* (New York: Harper & Brothers, 1938), pt. I.

formalism of the Established Church; which in the appeal it carried to emotion provided the needed delivery from the confines of Rationalism; and which in its ethical demands stirred the longings of the people and challenged the evil of the day. Some of its roots were to be found in the intense personal pietism of the German Moravians; but it had its main source in the experience of spiritual awakening which came to Wesley himself. As a result, it was ever clear to him that the force of religion is to be felt upon the individual character. "You must be born again" was the center of the revival, and the source of the rebirth was a compelling personal experience of Christ. "True religion is 'the life of God in the soul of man, bearing good fruit in every good work for human betterment.' "[10] The famous dictum that "the Gospel of Christ knows of no Religion but Social; no Holiness but Social Holiness,"[11] indicates the effect of this rebirth upon the individual. It was not only a matter of individual righteousness; it was a personal conversion of which the essential fruits were outgoing love and service.

The social results of the revival were widespread. Wesley's main appeal was to the workingmen of Britain, and the most fundamental result of it was the literal transformation of the character of the working class. Hitherto oppressed, poverty stricken, degraded in every way, they now as a result of the new life which was everywhere becoming apparent achieved a new sense of dignity. The exaltation of work and the emphasis upon thrift which were a large part of the Methodist moral code, served to create a new industriousness and prosperity.

[10] *Ibid.*, p. 296.

[11] John and Charles Wesley, *Hymns and Sacred Poems*, 5 ed., p. v. Through Wellman J. Warner, *The Wesleyan Movement in the Industrial Revolution*, (New York: Longman's, Green and Company, 1930), pp. 211-12.

Although it was Wesley's constant teaching that a man should not retain more money than was necessary to supply him with the necessities of life, and should give the rest away, this was an injunction hard to control. Methodism in a relatively short time became wealthy. Moreover, the rapid developments in the industrial revolution provided both incentive and opportunity for the exercise of the new industriousness. The high value which Wesley placed on the home as the natural environment for the development and nurture of religion resulted in greater stability there, with attendant control over sex life and over the prevailing drunkenness. If there had been a longing for moral probity during the period of great corruption, this was now converted into a positive transformation in character of the great masses of English industrial life.

In addition, there were specific reforms. The high view of human personality implicit in the revival made necessary organized attack upon oppression. Methodist local preachers were the first to organize unions of farmers, and the Methodists active in the beginnings of the trade union movement were legion; at the outset, the debt of the British Labor Party to Methodism was heavy. Moreover, Wesley's social conception of religion provided the incentive for organized relief of many types, for increased attention to public health and the care of the sick, and for prison reform. The distinctive contribution, however, at these points was not in the realm of new methods and conceptions. It was rather in the "strength of the humane attitude which it generated in the community."[12] Less of a reform than a new movement, however, was the development of education. It is in the Wesleyan revival that the foundations of public education in Britain were laid.

Not the least of the social achievements of Methodism came

[12] Wellman J. Warner, *op. cit.*, pp. 236-37.

indirectly. Both in the nonconforming and in the National churches, among the younger clergy and laymen alike there were evidences of the influence of the revival. Among those who were known as the Evangelicals, however, there arose a vigor of social concern and direct effectiveness which has rarely been paralleled. The names of Wilberforce and Shaftesbury alone are sufficient to recall the achievements wrought by these men. Although the ground swell of protest against chattel slavery had long been in force, enlarged substantially by the early Methodist protest against it, it was Wilberforce and his associates who achieved the abolition of it through law. And although the leaven had long been working both in the industrial classes and among those in power, it is to the efforts of Shaftesbury and his associates that the laws which brought about the virtual emancipation of industrial England were due.[13] The Evangelicals were not confined to any one church; yet they explicitly and repeatedly acknowledged that their vision and determination came from the warmth and power of evangelical Christianity. Here the influence of Methodism had become nearly complete: from its general permeation of individual character had arisen those who crystallized the gains into positive reform of the social structure.

From this contribution of Methodism, we turn lastly to the influence of Protestantism upon democracy. It must be at once recognized that democracy does not have its sole origin in Protestantism. Conceptions of natural law derived alike from ancient Stoicism and the eighteenth-century Enlightenment had a large influence, as did the conception of human rights held by the nineteenth-century Utilitarians. Nevertheless, the influence of Protestantism has been significant in the shaping of both democratic ideals and institutions.

[13] J. Wesley Bready, *op. cit.*, p. 388.

This influence has been in large part through the effect of basic Protestant concepts on the development of democratic philosophy. The worth of the individual, freedom, justice and a sense of community are all necessary ingredients of the democratic ideal.[14] They are also conceptions which stem directly from the Christian faith. The direct relationship to God which is at the heart of Protestantism, leads, as we saw in the case of the Wesleyan revival, to a sense of individual dignity and human worth. It means also that Christians must be free: free of those influences which may prevent or stifle such a direct relationship, and free to develop in it. The flowering of the Christian life under God can brook no political or social impediments. Moreover, the sweeping Protestant claim that *all* men may in principle be directly related to God, implies a demand for justice and an end to oppression lest the privilege be in fact denied to the many and open only to a few. Man not only stands in a direct spiritual relation to God; he has been created by God, and all men have been created by God. Here is the equalitarianism which is the root both of the democratic conception of justice and of community. Democracy implies a solidity of interests and a give and take of social intercourse which rests upon a more profound understanding of the human community. In large part this has been supplied by the Christian assertion that all men are the children of God. It has also been supplied by the experience of men in the Church: here is, in conception at least, that social solidarity which is the essence of brotherhood. From these two sources, on the one hand the sense of equality and on the other hand

[14] For an excellent discussion see George F. Thomas, "Christianity and Democracy," in *The Vitality of the Christian Tradition*, George F. Thomas, ed. (New York: Harper & Brothers, 1945), to which this section is largely indebted.

the sense of brotherhood resulting from the knowledge of a common Creator and the conception of the Christian community, come the democratic standards of justice and of human solidarity. It is true also, particularly in the United States, that the Church supplied men with their initial experience of democracy. Church government, whether of the congregational or the representative types, provided the daily experience which is fundamental to the working of political democracy.

One cannot help but be impressed with the nonpolitical character of the contribution of Protestantism to democracy. The legacy has not been primarily in terms of political theory. Indeed, the political thinking of the Reformers was predominantly authoritarian. On the contrary, the contribution has been made through the influence of the distinctive Protestant interpretation of the Gospel. It has been the derivatives of the theological conceptions of the priesthood of all believers, of Creation, and of the Church which have been determinative for the growth of democracy.

This is in fact the common bond among each of the three examples which we have been discussing. In each there has been a divergence between fundamental aim and result. The one has been the source of the other. Monasticism, Wesleyanism and Protestantism in general have been attempts to recapture the essence of the Gospel for their respective ages. They have been concerned at heart with the relation between man and God. Yet they have had far-reaching, and at first unlooked for, social results. A higher culture, social reform and political theory and structure have been the derivatives. In this is the justification of our original thesis: social transformation is the result, but only the result, of the basic work of the Church in evangelism. For if evangelism is the implanting of the Gospel in the hearts of the people, each of the movements we have been dealing with is in the broadest sense an evangelistic movement. The interest of each has been just at this point, and from them have come social results of far-reaching character.

(4) *The primacy of the Gospel means that the Church carries a responsibility for all men and not any particular section of society.* The Gospel asserts that there is one God who is the Creator of all and who has revealed Himself uniquely in Jesus Christ. The Gospel is, therefore, universal. It is universal in the sense, first, that it is the Truth concerning God and man's relation to Him. Christianity is thus from one viewpoint exclusive: its very claim to universality means that it cannot accommodate any other philosophy of different pre-suppositions and content. Whatever may have been the points of contact between Christianity and other philosophies in the past, and however it may have borrowed and incorporated into its own teaching insights from them, it has always maintained this exclusive character. Perhaps the most dramatic evidence of *rapprochement* between Christianity and non-Christian thought was in relation to Greek philosophy. Neither Plato, Aristotle nor the Stoics were wholly determinative in subsequent Christian theology. The systems of Augustine and of Aquinas, although they provided effective syntheses of Plato and Aristotle with Christianity and were influenced by them, nevertheless began and ended with the truth of the Christian revelation. The same is true for Christianity in the modern era. It cannot in principle approach any of the competing movements or religions in a spirit of eclecticism.[15] However it may co-operate on particular projects of worth, and to whatever degree it may modify its expressions and methods, Christianity, if it is to be true to its genius, must retain its universal

[15] See Vol. II, particularly Hugh Vernon White, chap. 9.

claim to Truth. "Hear O Israel, the Lord Thy God is One God" is not a faith which can tolerate rivals.

The Gospel is universal in another sense, namely, in that it is intended for all men. The Church is the Body of Christ: "Here there cannot be Greek and Jew, circumcised and un-circumcised, barbarian, Scythian, slave, free man, but Christ is all, and in all" (Colossians 3:11). Christianity is not a national or a tribal or a racial religion: The central concept is that "God so loved the *world* . . ."

The universal character of the Gospel means that the ulti-mate responsibility of the Church is for all of mankind. Truth cannot, unless it be denied, be contained within the boundaries of any one segment of society, nor any part of the world. Nor can Christ be confined to a particular group. Richard Niebuhr has made clear the nature of the responsibility of the Church.[16] The Church is responsible to God; that is, the account which it must ceaselessly render in its worship and in its work, is to the infinite Being whom it recognizes as the Author of life. More specifically, the Church is responsible to God-in-Christ, ". . . to the universal, absolute and unconditioned in the partic-ular . . ."[17] It is, in other words, in the double fact of the revelation of the universal God in Jesus and the sole allegiance which the Church owes to Him, that the universal *scope* of the Church's responsibility is to be found. Moreover, the *content* of this responsibility is discovered at precisely the same point. To the loyalty which the Church owes to God-in-Christ is added a loyalty to Christ-in-God; a loyalty which means that the life of the Church will, if it be true to its faith, exhibit that uni-versal love and mercy which are at the center of Jesus' life,

---

[16] Vol. III, chap. 5.
[17] *Ibid.*, p. 8.

and which are the core of the redemptive principle in the Christian revelation.

So to define the responsibility of the Church is to say that it must exert all its energies in all directions simultaneously. It cannot seek justice for one group at the unjust expense of or to the neglect of another. It cannot, for instance, by the weight of its institutional life associate itself with the privileged sections of society and adequately fulfill its responsibility. Nor can it throw its influence behind the proletariat with a view to securing their sole benefit. The dominantly priestly and pastoral concern of American Protestantism[18] is a denial of full responsibility, for it neglects the injustice done to vast sections of the population, all composed of individuals for each of whom Christ died. The association of the Church with the white race is perhaps the most flagrant denial of universal responsibility, exceeded only by the view of large sections of the laity and the ministry of the Church that the Gospel is really not true after all since one man's religion is as good as another's. To withhold justice from any, to overemphasize a partial ministry to the Church, to associate the Gospel with a single race or with a few of the nations of the earth, withholding it from all, is to deny the full responsibility which the Church owes to God and to Christ. A church which pursues one of these courses, or any other course of irresponsibility, is by that fact living in denial of that which it uniquely possesses. It has ceased to be a church, for it is explicit that the Gospel is universal and that the Church in which it lives has a universal responsibility for mankind.

It remains to draw together the four propositions which we have been discussing, and to ascertain their meaning for the

[18] James H. Nichols, Vol. I, pp. 21-23.

function of the Church. As a whole, they yield the following guiding concept which may be expressed in four parts:

(1) *The Church possessing uniquely a gospel of reconciliation is the soul of the world.* It is the Church which gives life to mankind. To speak thus is obviously to deal in the most ultimate terms. Human life will presumably go on without the Church, as it did for centuries previous to the existence of the Church. But the difference between life without the Church, which is to say life without the Gospel and without Christ, and life in the Church, is as great as the difference between the rational existence of man and the life of animals. The possession of reason by man means that he is distinguished from the beasts largely by the ability, through reason, to transcend both himself and his environment. He is capable of reflection, of analysis and of manipulation. He has been able to produce a civilization and a series of them by virtue of this distinguishing characteristic. Yet he has notoriously been unable to regulate with any appreciable degree of satisfaction that which is the nerve of the whole. The moral order, upon which the use of reason and the direction of civilization depend, has not been subject to the dictates of reason. The panaceas of philosophy have not been able to control the perversities of man's will. The consequence is that he lives a life which is not true life; it is but the merest foretaste of life. The beasts can walk and forage and manage their young; man with reason can construct and organize and set himself about with things and can even devise systems of thought and symphonies of music; but because he lacks the crucial element, he is as far removed from full life as is the beast from the life of reason.

It is the Gospel which animates life. It is the Gospel which puts in its proper perspective the reason of man and its achievements. It is the Gospel which carries the power to straighten the crookedness of the human will, and to provide the moral life (moral life, that is, in its widest connotation, which involves the loyalty to which obedience is given) with the direction it so desperately needs. It is the Gospel which provides redemption for men who are equipped by nature only with reason as a help, and who thus far have found no help in it. It is the Gospel which in lifting men from immoral into moral life, lifts them from death into the realm of eternal life. It is the Gospel which provides a dimension to life which is as distinctive and which is as profound in its importance as that dimension which is provided by reason, and upon which the ultimate effectiveness of reason wholly depends.

The Church which possesses this Gospel uniquely is thus the soul of the world. It is in the Church that the new dimension is found by men and cultivated until it ultimately becomes the controlling dimension of all living. This is, of course, not to say that it is in the churches, those faulty and human institutions with which we deal, that the Gospel and the full life are to be found exclusively. The Church is not the same as the churches. Many sections of the churches are devoid of the Gospel, and the Gospel lives outside the churches as well. Of this, human beings cannot be the judges, for "judgment is mine, saith the Lord." The Church which is the soul of the world is that spiritual community, established among us by the loving and merciful God, in which the Spirit of Christ reigns and binds men together.

Faulty as the human institutions which profess allegiance to this Church are, however, they are nevertheless the instruments through which the Gospel is proclaimed to men. It is upon the churches primarily that we must rely, and it is through them that we must work, in order to insure that the Gospel may impart its life to men. It is through the churches

that the basic function of the Church is performed. This function is evangelism: the imparting of that distinctive quality of
life which the Gospel alone can give and which provides life
itself with life. The Church as the soul of the world works in
the world in order that the world may have life. Its function
is evangelism.

(2) *The vigorous pursuit of evangelism leads to the creation
of a society modified by Christianity, namely, the development
of Christendom.* This happens in two ways. First, and most
profoundly, the extension of the Christian faith itself leads to
the permeation by it of the processes and structures of society,
with resultant effect upon them. Men who are truly possessed
by the Gospel will seek to alter their daily work in order that
it may conform more closely to Christian demands. Families
for whom Christ is the center of life will find their whole
conception of family life changed by His love. Governments
which rule predominantly Christian peoples will be much
modified by that fact. Moreover, the existence of the Christian
gospel among men will lead to direct, corrective responses to
injustice. Movements will be started, as they have been in the
past and as they are in the present, for the alleviation of
poverty and oppression and gross immorality. Specific laws will
be passed; reforms will be instituted. The success of the general
permeation of Christian influence through men's vocations and
their family life, as well as the effectiveness of the specific
reforms which are instituted, are, of course, inevitably qualified by the size and the strength of the Christian community
which constitutes them. In some instances, as in the case of
modern China, the influence of Christianity is in great dispro-
portion to the size of the Church. Yet in general, the constructive and ameliorative influence of the Church will depend upon

the effectiveness and extensiveness with which the fundamental task of evangelism is performed.

Success is qualified also by a different factor. This is the fact that the Christian faith is never fully exemplified by any type of social organization or civilization. The social extension of the faith is always approximate; that is, it must always be involved in compromises which fall short of the goal. Men, though they be loyal to the Gospel, are still limited in wisdom and they will sin; social institutions exhibit rigidities which prevent their easy and quick change for the better, and which prevent also the full expression of the justice and love toward which Christianity strives. Moreover, particularly in the case of the modern state, they are involved in a necessary regard for self-preservation and to some extent self-extension lest they perish. The solutions which we seek for our social ills must be recognized as proximate solutions only; "Christendom" is a term which signifies a modification of society by the Gospel, and not a complete fulfillment of its demands.

We have been accustomed to associate "Christendom" with the West, and with the civilization which the West has produced. Relatively recent developments, however, force a modification of this conception. The Church, as we shall have occasion to indicate more fully later on, has become a worldwide institution. It is no longer confined to the West, even though its predominant strength may continue to lie there. This means, however, that we can no longer think sectionally of Christendom. In the future the general permeation of culture and society by Christianity will not be in evidence primarily with reference to one culture or society. We are increasingly moving into an era in which the Church exists in a succession of cultures, some predominantly Western, some Oriental with Western influences, some still primitive. Each of these is now, and will be more in the future, modified by the Church. Christendom, therefore, is a more inclusive concept, meaning now and increasingly in the future, a series of cultures, each modified by Christianity, each containing a common Christian core, but each by virtue of its differences from the others, manifesting a different character. It may well be doubted whether we shall see the emergence of a culture embodying in modern terms the specific type of unity of the Middle Ages. The world character of the Church means that Christendom will involve not one uniform culture, however that might be conceived, but a number of differing societies, held together by a central faith.

The permeation of society by the Christian faith is not, however, an automatic matter. Although evangelism alone provides the base from which Christendom may arise, this is a matter of studied and determined effort. Wilberforce could not have succeeded had it not been for the influence throughout England of the Methodist revival; but his courageous and incisive legislative strategies were necessary for the final abolition of chattel slavery. This illustrates the second function of the Church, which is—to use the current term—social action. It is a function which is discharged in the legislative halls and in the labor unions; in the factories and in the universities; in the banks and in the courts of law. The churches may give broad directives and may issue judgments derived from the Gospel. But the implementation of these directives and these judgments takes place outside of the churches. Because this is so there is no reason for the churches to assume that they have no responsibility in this sphere. Social action is a function of the Church, and the responsibility, therefore, of the churches for concerted, deliberate and continuous action is extended to this realm with an urgency equal to, because it is derived from, their responsibility for evangelism.

(3) *The responsibility of the Church for all men sets as its goal for humanity the development of world community.* Religiously speaking, the goal of world community means nothing less than that the Gospel shall rule in the hearts of all men. This is the goal which Jesus himself has set: "Thy kingdom come." We need not repeat that the kingdom of God is universal in its scope. Every human is potentially a citizen in this kingdom, and the Church cannot rest until all of humanity actually is.

Sociologically speaking, the goal of world community means the establishment of a spiritual loyalty which will give cohesiveness and basic unity to the different cultures of the world. In this sense, world community is the basis for the emerging Christendom of which we have just been speaking. The urgency of the goal is apparent not only because of the nature of the Gospel. It is made indelible in our minds by the wars we have been through and the threat of wars which still hangs over our heads. Whether mankind will destroy itself through warfare is ultimately a matter of faith; we do not know whether it will be permitted to do so by its Creator. But we do know that the tools are at hand. The writing is on the wall, and the reply to it has been given to us. This reply is to be written "on the inward parts," and consists of that spiritual loyalty which, developed with power among the spirits of men, will make of them all a unity of brotherhood. It is this unity which is the essence of world community, and the constructive cohesiveness of the nations and the economies and the races and the cultures depends upon the power of the Church in developing it.

(4) *Throughout, the Gospel stands as judge, guide and power.* It is the Gospel that is supreme. It is supreme over the Church, for it is that which gives the Church its life. It is supreme over the churches, for it is only the Gospel present in them which can justify their existence. This supremacy is one

of judgment. All that Christians do, and all that the Church does, must be constantly measured up to the Gospel. The method and scope and constancy of its evangelism; the vigor and justice of its social action; the comprehensiveness of its efforts toward world community—these all stand under the Gospel, to be corrected and to be judged by it. This supremacy is that of guidance. To no other source can Christians and the Church look for wisdom. This wisdom is the foolishness of God, but as the early Christians and the subsequent heroes of the faith have so well demonstrated for us, it is wiser than the wisdom of the world, for it contains the power to transform human reason itself. This supremacy is that of power. In an age where physical power seems to be the all-important factor, we yearn for moral power to put our ideals into practice. Our task is to direct men and civilizations to faith in God, and it is not the power of the world which will accomplish this. Our reliance is upon the power of the Gospel, for we know that "it is God who worketh in us, both to will and to do."

3

THE ECUMENICAL REFORMATION

1. The existing churches: general description; special characteristics; the Church and the churches. 2. The ecumenical reformation: the unity of the Church; the world mission of the Church. 3. The vehicles of the reformation: The United States; the world scene. 4. The significance of the reformation: practical importance; world civilization; the Church.

FROM a description of the challenge which confronts Christianity in the modern scene and from a discussion of the basic function of the Church, we turn to an examination of the church situation today. What is the general context within which and out of which Christians must meet their challenge and exercise their function in the world?

It is the thesis of this chapter that the present church situation is characterized by the progress of a profound reformation. At the close of the Middle Ages, it was apparent that there was needed a fundamental reorientation in the life of the Church. Conditions were so far from the teachings of the Gospel, that the reconception and new life involved in the Protestant and Catholic Reformations were necessary to continued Christian effectiveness and fidelity to God. We are in a similar position. The actual conditions, of course, have changed. We are not called upon to protest the same evils as were the Reformers. The point of similarity, however, is in the fact that in the Church now, as then, there is neeeded a radical reformation, to the end that the Church may recapture its true character and fulfill its true mission.

This reformation is the ecumenical reformation. It is in process now and has been for perhaps as much as a century. It is already widespread in its effectiveness; yet it has far to go before completion. Though it has its influential leaders, it differs from the Protestant Reformation in that it has not been set in motion primarily by the leadership of great prophets. The historian of the ecumenical movement cannot look back upon one or two, as Protestants turn back to Luther and Calvin. The ecumenical reformation is the result rather of multitudinous voices and efforts, some of them organized and some of them unorganized, some of them conscious of the reform they were seeking and some wholly unconscious of it. In spite, however, of the length of its duration and its lack of decisive and towering prophets, its vigor and its importance for the Church should not be underestimated. Indeed, it may be just because of the implications of the slow tempo of its progress and the widespread nature of its leadership that it may be the most profound and far-reaching of the reformations which the Church has yet undergone.

To outline the character of the ecumenical reformation we shall need to examine briefly the churches as they exist without reference to the ecumenical movement, and then to turn to the ecumenical movement itself.

1. THE EXISTING CHURCHES

General description

The Christian churches may be classified as falling into three main groups:[1] Roman Catholic, Eastern Orthodox and

[1] See further Matthew Spinka, Vol. IV, chap 1. The present treatment is heavily indebted to this chapter.

Protestant. Although a strict classification would add the Anglican communion as a fourth, with much justification, the association of it with the Protestant bodies and its dissociation from the Church of Rome allow its legitimate inclusion under the term "Protestant." It will obviously not be possible to provide within our limited space any but the barest outlines, but we may have in mind some of the distinctive characteristics of each of these groups, as well as the parts of the world in which they are found.

The Roman Catholic Church is the dominant church in Italy, France, Poland, Austria, southern Germany, Belgium, Portugal, Spain, Eire, the Philippines and Latin America. It is a strong minority in Great Britain, Canada and the United States. There are indications that the Vatican considers the most important minority center of Catholicism, and perhaps even the most important center of it, to be the United States. The Roman Church has always been strongly missionary, and is to be found in most of the traditionally considered missionary lands, where it is a sizable minority and growing rapidly.

The most distinctive element in the faith of the Roman Church is its conception of the Church. The Roman Catholic Church *is* the Church; she is the Body of Christ.

> Christ himself endowed her, through Peter and his successors, the popes, with authority to rule all the faithful the world over; to dispense the sacraments which are channels of supernatural grace; and to guard the purity of truth which is contained not only in the Scriptures, but also in the tradition in her keeping. Accordingly, outside the Church there is no salvation, because there is no fullness of truth, or of sacramental grace, or of divine authorization to govern.[2]

[2] *Ibid.,* p. 38.

From the Council of Trent (1545-1563) until the present day, the tendency has been to consolidate this position, the climax being reached in 1870 with the declaration of the doctrine of papal infallibility. The doctrine is more important as an indication of the temper of the Church than as an article of faith, although it is that, for it is the symbol of the close-knit institution, in faith, organization and function, which the Roman Church has become.

Classical Protestantism developed in four forms:[3] Lutheran, Reformed, sectarian or radical, and Anglican. Luther's protest was aimed primarily at the establishment of a direct relationship between God and the individual, and this was secured through two basic concepts. He declared that, not the Church, but the Bible was the sole rule of faith and life, thus making access to the faith dependent upon the individual's understanding of the Scriptures. Moreover, he declared that no intermediaries were necessary between man and God, but that each person was his own priest. "The priesthood of all believers" involved the right and duty of each person to study and discern the word of God, which is the gospel of justification by faith within the scriptures.

Calvin was heavily indebted to Luther, but emphasized two matters which made the Reformed tradition different from Lutheranism. For Calvin the will of God was supreme and absolutely determinative for human life. Predestination is the characteristic mark of Calvinism, whether in Presbyterian or Baptist form. An insistence on ethical discipline, leading eventually to puritan morality, is also a distinguishing element in Calvinism. "Protestant radicalism" appeared in various forms, identifiable because they all conformed to the general characteristics of the "sect" as contrasted with the "church"

---

[3] See *Ibid.*, pp. 14 ff., and Albert C. Outler, "The Reformation in Classical Protestantism," in *The Vitality of the Christian Tradition.*

forms. Of this "left wing" of Protestantism, the Anabaptists were the most prominent. Their view involved an intensely personal religion, not subject to external authority of any kind, ecclesiastical or state. It is, on the whole, typical that they supported believers' (i.e., adult) baptism in their insistence upon the reality of religion for each individual.

It is characteristic of Anglicanism that it cannot be identified by a reference to a single person or statement or movement. It has affinities, both historical and inherent, to both Catholic and Protestant Christianity. Because of the different course of the Reformation in England from that on the Continent, much of Catholic tradition and thought was preserved. On the other hand, the influence of the continental Reformation has been profound. The official faith, embodied in the Thirty-nine Articles, the Prayer Book, and the historic episcopate are perhaps the most important identifying factors of Anglicanism. It should also be noted that in the mother country, England, it is a National Church, although in other countries it is found in separation from the state. Aside from its inherent qualities, the Anglican communion is important for the ecumenical movement because of its comprehensive character. Its insistence upon a catholic conception of the Church, its maintenance of the historic episcopate, and its continuity in thought and worship with the ancient church give it affinities with both Orthodox and Roman Catholicism. The modifications which Protestantism, particularly Calvinism and Methodism, have wrought upon it, and its intimate association with Protestant churches have provided even closer connections with the Protestant tradition.

Protestantism in America has run a diversified course, which is typified by the multiplication of the relatively few churches of the colonial days into over 250 denominations at the present. For the most part, it consists of variations of classical Protestantism which came to the country with immigrants, from the

Puritan fathers on. There have been some distinctively American denominations, of which the Disciples of Christ is the chief. The conditions surrounding the phenomenal expansion of Methodism in this country have given American Methodism, despite its British origin, many uniquely American characteristics. The separation of church from state has provided for an equality before the law which, combined with the toleration implicit in the democratic ideal, has made for an equalitarian temper among the churches. Although the Roman Catholic Church, some Lutheran bodies and some radically sectarian groups maintain an exclusive outlook, this is not typical. Moreover, the majority of the churches are homogeneous in outlook and in much of their worship. In addition to the multiplication of churches, the most characteristic element in American Protestantism is the prevailing similarity of church life.[4]

The dominant Protestant countries are Great Britain, the United States, Holland, the Scandinavian countries, northern Germany, Switzerland, Czechoslovakia, Canada, New Zealand and Australia. There are strong Protestant minorities in France and Hungary. Protestantism in the nineteenth century gave birth to the greatest missionary expansion the Church has ever known, and as a result may count "younger churches" in the Orient, Africa, Latin America and the Islands of the seas.

The main centers of Eastern Orthodoxy are in Russia, the Balkans and the Near East. The nineteen Eastern Orthodox churches are largely autonomous national bodies, bound together in a loose fellowship. There is an ecumenical patriarch, but this is an honorary office, and he is in no sense an "Eastern pope." The doctrinal unity of the Orthodox churches is embodied in the pronouncements of the seven ecumenical councils (325-787).

[4] H. Paul Douglass, Vol. IV, pp. 10-11.

In essence, these pronouncements consist of the doctrine of the Incarnation—that God revealed Himself in a true human body, soul and spirit—the Trinitarian doctrine, asserting that the one divine substance is known to the human mind under three hypostases or aspects; and the doctrine of the two natures, divine and human, comprising the one person of Jesus Christ.[5]

Further unity is provided by canons, or regulations, which govern the polity of the churches. Within these limits, the autonomous, or autocephalous churches as they are more properly called, are free to govern themselves. To a great extent these churches have taken on the marked characteristics of their cultures and have, both by virtue of this and by virtue of their near subservience to the state, become national churches. Fundamental to the Orthodox churches, however, is their doctrine of the Church. This is the doctrine of *Sobornost*, in essence a doctrine that the Church is the communion of those who possess the spirit of Christ. For its relations with other bodies of Christendom, this doctrine, together with the fact that there is no single comprehensive and binding creed, is the most important aspect of Eastern Orthodoxy.

Special characteristics[6]

It is important to add to this description of the churches *as churches* some comments upon them *as institutions*. The full story is not told by a brief, or indeed even a full, description of the faith of the churches; their life is determined with

[5] Matthew Spinka, Vol. IV. p. 28.

[6] From this point on, we shall be almost exclusively concerned with Protestantism, and use the term "Church" in its Protestant meaning. The justification for this is in the facts that the Roman Church excludes itself from the ecumenical reformation, which is our main concern, and that, although Eastern Orthodoxy has been friendly to the ecumenical movement, the Russian Church, about which very little is known of its contemporary life, exerts a heavy influence.

almost equal force by their character as institutions. For it is in their character as organized institutions, owning property, possessing a membership, employing people, carrying on a program, that they are subject to the same social forces which affect other social institutions. We are not primarily concerned with an analysis of the manner in which they are so affected, but rather with a broad recognition of some of the more important results of this fact.

It is clear that the Protestant churches are primarily Western institutions. It is within the culture of the West that they have had their origin, and in which they have grown and multiplied. Moreover, it is industrialized culture—in which commerce and the nation-state are dominant—that has formed their social environment. Although the nineteenth-century missionary enterprise has resulted in the development of churches which are native to non-Western cultures, these are still so young and in such a minority in their respective lands as to modify the prevailing Western character of the churches only slightly. Moreover, it was inevitable that the missionaries should take and teach the customs which were habitual with them, and it is only with difficulty that the "younger churches" are able to modify these importations. Without in the least disparaging the significance for both the present and particularly the future of the "younger churches," it is nevertheless clear that Protestant church life at present is predominantly Western.

To explore the significance of this fact fully would necessitate an examination of it church by church and country by country. Some general factors may, however, be pointed out. The first of these is the accommodation of the church to a society dominated by bourgeois capitalism. The main characteristics of this society have been outlined in the first chapter; the accommodation of the churches to them has been in their organizational management, ideology and membership. The management of ecclesiastical enterprise has been, by and large, according to the accepted business standards of the day. The churches have not hesitated to hold property, not only as is required for their own use, but also as investment. The vast sums at their disposal in the form of endowments have been invested in commercial enterprise. The disparity of wages common in the industrial scene has been reproduced among their employees. Although criticisms of the various more flagrant abuses of the economic system have been frequent and specific, particularly in Britain and the United States, the basic concepts of the churches have been in support of it. The sanctity of private property, the conviction that competition would automatically secure the most equitable distribution of the world's goods, and the necessity of guaranteeing individual initiative, have been the bulwarks of Protestant economic ethics. With the growth of Methodism in Great Britain into a middle-class church, and with the disappearance of the frontier in the United States, the membership of the churches has been predominantly middle class. The one exception is that of the Negro churches of the United States, which are overwhelmingly of lower-income groups, and which tend to correct the overall picture for Protestantism in the United States.

However, in the membership of local churches and of particular denominations, and in leadership, its middle-class character—typical of bourgeois capitalism—cannot be denied.[7] This has meant, of course, that large benefits have accrued to the institutional life of the churches. Middle-class members have been able to place more money at their disposal, and the missionary, educational and literature programs have profited accordingly. The large educational opportunities open to the

[7] John C. Bennett, Vol. III, p. 146 ff.

children of middle-class homes have meant that the churches could achieve an educated ministry and in great measure an educated laity. The churches have, to a large extent to their benefit, shared the general prosperity of industrialized society. On the other hand, this is the most pervasive evidence of secularism in the churches. They have not been able to show the increasing transcendence of their economic environment which would result in consistent judgment of it and efforts to transform it; on the contrary, the influence of secular economic life and thought have shown an increasing ascendancy over the churches.

A second special characteristic is the degree to which national consciousness—also a marked feature of Western civilization—has affected the churches. As those who attend international church gatherings frequently testify, it is possible to discern an American and a French and a German and a British type of Christianity. This is shown in very generalized characteristics, none of which is completely typical of any particular church within a nation, but all of which have their influence upon the total church life. The most obvious example is the contrast between the general social activism, the tendency to associate Christianity with democracy, the lack (until recently) of consuming interest in theological questions, and the multiplicity of denominational expressions which are typical of American Christianity; and the socially passive, homogeneous and theologically sophisticated Lutheranism of Germany. That these predominantly national characteristics develop into a national church consciousness is indicated by two facts. The first is the attitude of the churches to war; in World War I there was a virtual identification of the cause of the churches with the cause of the nation; in World War II the situation was vastly different owing to the persecution of the church in Germany which set it in opposition to the state, and owing to the advanced position of the leadership of the churches of the allied nations which refused to make such a simple identification as had been done previously. Throughout the rank and file of church membership, however, the association of the cause of the church and of the nation seemed to be more real, particularly in the United States. Evidence for this fact is not only in prevailing popular opinion, but also in the treatment of the conscientious objectors, who, although they were provided for by law, were largely neglected by all but the traditionally peace churches. Although church leaders stood behind them, the money necessary for their support was not forthcoming, making it clear that their position could not be understood by the general membership of the churches. The second evidence of national consciousness appears in America and on the mission field. It is not uncommon in both areas to see individual churches of the same communion, but of different national backgrounds, existing side by side, without the thought of union, and indeed with considerable resistance to it. Swedish, Norwegian and German Lutherans will all be found in American cities, all separate; American Episcopalians and British Anglicans are similarly at work in the same mission field. Whereas the formation of national characteristics in the churches has in part a unifying tendency, as in the homogeneity of American Christianity, it also produces divisions within the churches.

A third characteristic important for our purposes is the prevalence and depth of racism in the churches.[8] The exclusive historical association of the Church with the West has resulted in the identification of it with the white race, with the result that the churches were by so much more open to the inroads of racism. There were not within the fellowship those blocs

[8] See Buell G. Gallagher, Vol. I, chap. 4.

of representatives of other races which would have prevented
or at least modified the encroachments of racial theories and
feelings into church life. However one may analyze the rise of
racism, whether as being due to this association of Christianity
with the white race, or as resulting from factors outside of the
church, or from a combination of these, the fact remains that
as racism gained force within the context of Western civilization, the white constituency of the churches provided fertile
ground for its growth even within the Body of Christ. The
fruit of this growth is evident on every hand. One searches far
and wide for genuinely interracial churches, that is, in both
membership and ministry, and those few which do exist are
hailed as "significant experiments." Christianity has, to be
sure, not been withheld from those of other races, but it has
been given to them in isolation. "The only possible institutional
rival of the Protestant church in America for the dubious
honor of being most thoroughly Jim Crow in its practices is
the less enlightened wing of trade unionism."[9] The spectacle
of Negro churches and white churches is devastating enough;
the effect which both segregation and the racial superiority of
the white man which it implies has upon Christians is equally
destructive. There is hardly a more disheartening sight
than the reaction of a substantial and earnest white congregation, honestly striving for the righteousness of the Lord,
to the Christian demand for racial inclusiveness. It is only
rarely that this reaction is positive; the prevailing temper of
it is defensive, whether this takes the form of violence or of
quiet determination. In this defensiveness, which is a reflection
of the general defensiveness of the white race so well outlined
for us by Gunnar Myrdal,[10] there is evident active resistance to

[9] *Ibid.,* p. 99.
[10] Gunnar Myrdal, *An American Dilemma,* 2 vols. (Harper & Brothers,
1944). See especially pts. I and II.

one of the clearest demands of the Christian ethic. It is virtually an effort to serve two masters, and so powerful and pervasive is the loyalty to white supremacy—however it may be expressed—that it thwarts the responsiveness of Christians to their loyalty to God in other areas of life. Here is a strait jacket upon our souls: an involvement in the individual and collective guilt of injustice done to neighbors on a grand scale, which stifles the vitality of the Church in all that it does. In Europe the churches resisted at great cost the Nazi demand for anti-Semitism, and experienced forthwith a new vitality which extended throughout their whole life; here is constructive evidence of the suffocating burden which submission to racism places upon us. This reaction to anti-Semitism is one of the most hopeful signs in regard to this problem in the West. Though it can hardly be said that anti-Semitism is completely gone from all European church life, the recovery of righteousness on this point which marked the resistance to the Nazis carries large promise for continued reform. There is, moreover, an awakening in the United States, particularly on the part of the leadership of the churches. And as we shall shortly see, the presence within the world fellowship of Christians of the "younger churches" of Africa and the Orient is a force which may be our salvation. Yet in spite of these signs of hopefulness, the power of racism over church life in the West cannot be minimized.

The various accommodations which the Church has had to make to its surrounding culture cannot be treated lightly. Because of the fact that the Church is embodied in institutions of vast scope, it is inevitably subject to those influences which compose its social milieu. It is as impossible to expect that the churches could hold aloof from bourgeois capitalism and nationalism and racism as it is to suppose that the church of the Middle Ages could be separated from feudalism and the

Holy Roman Empire. Yet to admit the inevitability of entangle-
ment with the environment is not to excuse the churches from
the sins which they commit because of it. Racism is no less a
sin because it has come upon a Church native to a caste-con-
trolled society. Capitalism is no more essential to the Christian
ethic than feudalism, and the identification of the Church with
it no less sinful than the identification of the Church with any
other economic system. It is at this point that judgment and
repentance are most insistently called for in institutional life:
judgment in order that the secularism of the churches may be
the more clearly discerned, and repentance in order that there
may be continuous efforts at disentanglement and reform.

The Church and the churches

The multiplicity of the denominations of Christendom is
perhaps its most immediately striking feature. These range
from the various types of contemporary sects,[11] some of which
are only on the fringe of the Christian movement, to the great
churches by which central Christianity is defined. Some of the
denominations take their stand on particular ethical issues, as
in the case of the historic peace churches. Others stem as we
have seen directly from the Reformation. Still others have had
their rise as a result of such peculiarly national characteristics
as the American frontier, and from such distinctively religious
phenomena as the eighteenth- and the nineteenth-century
revivals. Whatever their origin, each of these churches is a
self-conscious body, possessing a definite creed or accepted
system of beliefs and a separate institutional life. They are all
subject to the prevailing cultural trends which we have been
describing.

This diverse character of the churches has served an impor-

[11] See Pierson Parker, Vol. II, chap. 8.

tant function. It has allowed for the expression of distinctive temperaments and concerns and has provided the avenue for the fulfillment of particular conceptions of Christian vocation. The difference, for instance, between the liturgical and the "free" churches, indicates not only a divergence in tradition, but a response to those whose desire for worship is best expressed in either of these two broad forms. The full Christian revelation will inevitably impress persons in different ways: for some the indwelling Spirit of Christ is all important; for others the majesty and power of the will of God is primary; for still others the experience of radical conversion seems necessary; and for yet another group the gradual nurture of the Christian spirit is normal. In large part the origin of the different churches may be explained in terms of responses to these needs; and clearly their existence provides the means whereby they may be satisfied. This has meant, in turn, that the effectiveness of the Church as a whole has been enhanced by the variations in its institutional life. Denominationalism in one of its aspects is the process whereby the Church has "become all things to all men." In so doing it has secured an extensiveness of outreach, in turn increasing its impact upon the world.

On the other hand, in at least three important ways, the diversity of the churches is an immense handicap. First, it has fostered a spirit of exclusiveness among Christians. Historically and on the present scene Christians have been notoriously unable to assert that which is important to them, and allow others to do the same. They have found it necessary to ascribe to their distinctive interpretations the character of absolute truth, to the end that those who found themselves in disagreement were virtually excluded from the Christian fellowship. This has been true of the more extreme form of theological

and Biblical conservatism, the one insisting on agreement
with a particular creed, the other on acceptance of the literal
and word-for-word truth of the Bible. It reaches its climax,
however, in the attitude toward the Lord's Supper. So large
have been the gains made in the establishment of unity at the
Lord's Table that the majority of the Protestant churches
practice some degree of open communion. Yet within a few,
indeed some of the most important, churches there is a rigid
exclusiveness which prevents the recognition that the Sacrament administered by ministers of other churches has a regu-
larity or effectiveness or validity which is equal to their own
administration of it. The effect of this is to deny to members
of other churches the Sacrament unless they change their
church membership. It need hardly be said that this exclusiveness at the Lord's Table strikes at the crucial point, for it is
here that Christian worship and brotherhood are intended to
find their highest expression. Such an attitude also forms the
crux of Christian disunity. Disunity does not consist primarily
in the fact of a multiplicity of organizations. They can, as we
shall presently see, form among themselves a large measure
of unity, with the result that there is a unified diversity wholly
beneficial to the Church. Disunity, however, lies in the fact
that Christians exclude one another from the fundamental
Christian fellowship, and allow this seriously to affect their
common work in the world. The result is that the Church is
lost among the churches, and the Body of Christ is dismem-
bered into separate units which both in outward form and in
inward reality have no common center.

A second handicap found in the diversity of the churches is
in the dissipation of energy which results. Everywhere there
is an almost scandalous overlapping and duplication of effort.
Here are a dozen of the larger denominations. Each has its

separate government, program, administration, budgets. Each has its board of foreign missions and its board of home missions and its board of education; its Sunday-school work; its young people's headquarters; and its social action division. For each there are the great councils and the lesser councils with their executives and their program directors. Money is raised and spent, people are hired and meetings are held, and their functions, and to a great extent the content of these functions, vary only a little from one denomination to another. With all the accommodation which the churches have made to current business practice, here is one area in which their management has, to its detriment, made a successful protest. In all of the vaunted efficiency of American life, the most glaring example of inefficiency is in the overall management of ecclesiastical institutions. This is, of course, not the result of neglect or willful design. It is the result of the evolution of the pattern of denominationalism, and those who are now caught in its inefficient web are quite helpless. Of the practical effects of diversity, the dissipation of financial, organizational and human energy is the most serious. It is also one of the most perplexing, for there are good reasons for hesitating to adopt an overall organization of church life. Protestants are jealous of their freedom, and centralization of institutional life, in the religious as well as in the economic or political sphere, is fraught with danger for this precious possession. This danger, however, should not blind us to the disastrous waste which is involved in it.

The third handicap is in the confusion of tongues which is presented to the world by the many churches. The world desperately needs and deeply longs for a decisive word. But facing it are a multiplicity of churches, the differences among which not only prevent a unified voice, but which when they are explained convey an impression of such a complexity of involved argument that the inquiring non-Christian turns away in confusion. It is not only that the Presbyterians claim one thing and the Methodists another and the Quakers still something different. The essence of the difficulty is that the "distinctive" claims of the different churches are those which arose in a distantly past age, and which have little or no relevance to the contemporary scene. This is most tragically illustrated on the mission field, where men have been stirred by the vision of Christ, and have been taught the virtues of one intricacy of doctrine against another. The lack of a single Christian message is also at the root of the failure of the churches to devise a common strategy. Diversity has become not only a diversity of institutions and of thought and of worship; it has become the license for an un-co-ordinated and undisciplined attack upon the evils which beset the world. In some cases, notably in reference to government, a united strategy has been forced, because government will listen to nothing less than a united voice. But for the most part the world is presented with discordant voices and anxious scurryings in which there is no unity.

2. THE ECUMENICAL REFORMATION

Within this general scene there is in process a profound reformation. It is reformation which amid the disunity of the churches asserts the unity of the Church. It is a reformation which amid the provincialism of the churches asserts the world mission of the Church. It is a reformation born of the desires of a multitude of people, of a hundred different types of organized effort and in response to the spontaneous prayer of persons in all lands and churches.

The unity of the Church

The ecumenical reformation asserts the unity of the Church in the midst of the disunity of the churches. Fundamental to this assertion is the growing realization that Christ willed unity among his followers. To this we shall shortly return; suffice it to say here that at root the demand of the ecumenical reformation for unity is a response to the Master, growing from a new perception of his will for them. Another basic factor is an increasing sense of the importance of the Church.[12] We have noted in the first chapter that the dominant characteristics of our age are antithetical to the Gospel. The urgency with which this hostile world presses upon Christians has had the effect of driving them together, producing in their minds a realization that the fellowship of the Church is necessary, lest amid the forces of secularism their Christian witness perish. With this new recognition has come the discovery of the value of community, not only as a source of strength, but as a value in itself. For it is, as we have so long been told and been so little mindful, in a community of love with other men that our own spirits find their true harmony and development. This new sense of the fellowship of the Church has been accompanied by a rediscovery of the value of theology: men have turned to reflection upon the meaning of their Christian experience, and from this as well as from study of the ancient theologies of the Church have had their initial sense of the value of the Church strengthened. Social pressure and the teachings of theology have conspired to the same end. Moreover, there has been a clearer recognition that it is to the Church that we are indebted for all of the Christian tradition which makes our witness on the present scene possible. There

[12] John C. Bennett, Vol. IV, chap. II.

has been not only a new realization of the value of the present community of those who strive with us, but a sense of our solidarity with those of the past. We have come to recognize our place in a great stream of witnesses who, throughout past ages and the present time, have formed the community of the faithful. In addition, leaders of the churches, a few thousand of them, have been for the past half century associating with one another in great international conferences. While this experience has been limited to these few, it has had a large influence through them, for as men from the nations and the races gather together worshiping a common Lord, testifying to their diversity by their language and their customs and their color, yet witnessing to the God and Father of all, the reality of the fellowship of the Church has become apparent. This rediscovery at first hand, and out of the experience of multitudes, constitutes the very base of the ecumenical reassertion of unity. A knowledge of the spiritual community of the Church has led to an understanding that this community is one and undivided.

The efforts to translate this general sense of unity into practical results have taken five main forms.[13] Although the historical sequence of their appearance has roughly followed the logical sequence of their presentation here, it should be recognized that they have appeared in church life at different times and at different places. The following is more of a descriptive than a historical outline. We may mention the unity which has appeared in the forms of unofficial organizations, mutual recognition, federation, federal union and full corporate union.

(1) Christians from different churches have joined together in a large number of unofficial enterprises. One of these is a community of thought and worship. Most of the leading

[13] *Ibid.*, pp. 67 ff.

thinkers in the churches are not identifiable first by their denominational affiliation, and in part this is due to the interchange of opinion and fellowship which is constantly in process through informal meetings as well as through individual contact. The prevalence of interdenominational worship, and the use by persons of one church of worship booklets issued by another church are powerful contributors to this informal but real unity. Increasingly the development of theology and the vitality of worship cross denominational lines.

Another type of unofficial enterprise involves a wide-ranging group of organizations. Some of these have been temporary. Others have developed into large, permanent organizations. Many are nondenominational, organized without reference to the churches; still others have some type of direct relationship to churches and are interdenominational. The purposes of these multitudinous bodies are varied: the distribution of Bibles, the promotion of the missionary enterprise, the approach to youth, social reform, political influence, the development of Christian unity. Although a listing of the specific organizations and their interrelationships would present a complex picture in which unity would seem almost to be lost, each one and all taken together have been powerful factors in the growth of basic Christian unity. Individuals of differing view have been brought together; representatives of varied churches have been united in common pursuits. In the unofficial bodies, a ground swell has been created and found expression. In the process, two tendencies have been marked.[14] First, the evolution of informal, frequently temporary conferences and consultations into permanent organizations. Second, the tendency of agencies started by individual Christians to develop a closer and, in the majority

[14] Henry P. Van Dusen, *World Christianity, Yesterday, Today and Tomorrow* (New York: Abingdon-Cokesbury Press, 1947), chap. 3.

of cases, an organic relationship to official church bodies. It is these trends which have turned what might well have been but a series of sporadic efforts into a tangible contributor to unity among the churches.

(2) Mutual recognition is a term which has at once a broad and a specific meaning. In its broad sense, it is the very base of Christian unity, for it involves the admission that members of other churches are Christians, simply by the fact that they are members of churches. Mutual recognition does not demand conformity to a creed, whether of theological belief, Biblical interpretation or social conviction. It is the opposite of that exclusiveness which we saw to cut the nerve of Christian unity. Among those who are able to give mutual recognition to other Christians, convictions are not any the less firmly held, but there is a consciousness that these convictions do not have the ultimate status of the Gospel itself, but rather are judged by that Gospel. In this broad sense, mutual recognition is the basis of Christian unity.

In the more specific sense, however, mutual recognition refers to certain relationships between churches, and is a specialized form of Christian unity. It appears in interchange of membership, interchange of ministries, in intercommunion and in comity agreements. Each of these involves the recognition of the full Christian status of one church by another. Such a recognition then allows for members of one church to be transferred to another without further examination; for ministers without additional ordination to officiate in a church of another communion; for the Sacrament to be administered by the ministers and to the members of two or more communions without special dispensations; and for the division of geographical territory among the churches for the purposes of evangelism and church extension. It should be noted that in one form or another mutual recognition is already practiced by a large section of American Protestantism. It is not typical, however, of any large number of the churches in all its forms. Comity arrangements are the most prevalent; and intercommunion is the most difficult of achievement.

(3) The unity which results in federation is widespread; it is, in fact, the dominant contemporary expression of unity among the churches. It involves mutual recognition in its general sense, but goes further in that there is created a continuing organization of which different churches are members, usually under a constitution, and to which from time to time are delegated powers for specific purposes. Three major examples are the Federal Council of the Churches of Christ in America, the International Missionary Council and the proposed World Council of Churches. The advantage of these federations is obvious: they provide a common meeting ground for the official representatives of the churches, and a common avenue of action. The limitation (which may not be a disadvantage) of them is that they possess no power whatever save that which may be granted as occasion demands. Moreover, even in these cases, churches which dissent are not bound by the majority decision. That the federation has an indirect power of wide scope, however, cannot be denied. It is constantly in a position to exert leadership either in the direction of more unity within the federation or in different forms, and if it is wisely directed the momentum of its prestige carries a heavy weight. Although federation can by no means be regarded as the final expression of unity, it is an important and hopeful step on the way.

(4) Federal union. A comprehensive scheme of federal union has yet to be put into practice. In essence, however, it would keep the principle of federation and carry it one step further.

It would, as in the case of the federal government, delegate power to the federated body in order that it might make decisions governing the constituent members.

(5) Full corporate union, as the name implies, involves a merger of government, organization, ministry and function. In corporate union, two or more churches become one church. Whether it is a solution which is feasible or desirable for all of the churches of Christendom, even if they could be brought to the necessary point of agreement, is a matter of widespread debate. It is, however, an effective means of consolidating individual churches, and has been a powerful contributor to the growing realization of unity.

> [In the past one hundred and fifty years, specifically,] there have occurred no fewer than eighty-eight such unions. Some achieved merely mergers of closely related bodies, occasionally those which had earlier separated. Some involved comparatively small groups. Others were of vast scope and the highest significance. It is important to distinguish unions of so-called "related" communions, i.e., of the same general family (Presbyterian, Methodist, Lutheran, etc.) from unions of so-called "unrelated" families. Sixty-two were of the former type (e.g., the union of Presbyterians in Scotland, and of Methodists in the United States, England, China and Korea), but twenty-six brought together church bodies whose historic antecedents and usually their polities or doctrine were sharply contrasted (e.g., the United Church of Canada, the Evangelical and Reformed Church, the Church of Christ in China, the United Church of Northern India, the South India United Church, the Church of Christ in Japan, etc.). . . . All through the earlier decades of the period, the great bulk of unions was within denominational families. In the past two decades, the proportion has shifted sharply; the numbers of unions of related and those of unrelated churches are exactly equal. Com-

munions which have participated in mergers across family lines include Baptists, Congregationalists, Christians, Evangelicals, Methodists, Presbyterians, Reformed and United Brethren—all the major Protestant denominations, except Episcopalians and Lutherans.[15]

It is in such varied ways that the ecumenical reformation is in part expressed. To a large degree these five forms of unity themselves are important. These multiple organizations and plans have been the means whereby Christians have come to know one another and to value the contributions which others have to make. They have been the tangible evidence of the reality of the will to unity. They have been the testing ground on which the validity of different solutions has been worked out. Yet the contemporary forms of Christian unity are not the most fundamental matter. None of them is final; in no quarter is there complete satisfaction that the ultimate solution has been found. It is rather in the *basic spirit* which has brought them all into existence that their importance ultimately lodges. Here is the real reformation. For it is in this spirit that men have found anew the significance of the Spirit of Christ, whose unmistakable will for his followers was that they should live together in an unbroken community of love. It is in this new discovery that the Church is again beginning to emerge with power from the churches.

The world mission of the Church

The ecumenical reformation asserts not only the unity of the Church but also the world mission of the Church. It is in fact the assertion of the world mission of the Church which gives to the ecumenical reformation its most distinctive character. As John Bennett has pointed out,[16] it would be quite

[15] Henry P. Van Dusen, *ibid.*
[16] Vol. IV, p. 59.

possible to have a church which was united but took no interest in its universal responsibility. In the current reformation, however, the vision of a world mission and the drive toward its fulfillment have been distinctive. That this constitutes a reformation is undoubted. We have seen that the dominant institutional characteristics of the churches have been in the main limited to the West. We have also seen that they have, within Western culture of the modern period, tended to become typical of the middle class, rather than inclusive of all classes. It is against the prevailing provincialism of a Western middle-class orientation that the vision of a world mission is in protest. This assertion of world mission has three main expressions: world-wide evangelism, a comprehensive approach to society, and a conscious effort toward the creation of churches indigenous to their various cultures.

It cannot be our task to document the unprecedented missionary expansion of the churches of the nineteenth and twentieth centuries. The range and power of it, however, may be indicated by a symbolic event. In Amsterdam, Holland, four weeks before the outbreak of World War II there was convened a conference of Christians. Three aspects of this conference are of primary importance. It was, except for possibly the missionary conference at Madras in 1938, the most internationally representative meeting of any kind, religious or political, that had ever been held in the history of the race. It was a conference of young people primarily under thirty. Its rallying theme was *"Christus Victor."*

What lies behind these facts? First, they mean an outpouring of human lives running into the thousands and of money running into the millions. For the preceding hundred years and more, men and women, some of them the most able the Church has known, had voluntarily offered their lives for work in distant lands. These people had come from the New World and the Old; they were students from the universities and young people from the churches; they were professionally trained and they were persons of no particular skills. Behind them stood the interest and the money and the prayers of the peoples of the churches of the homelands. All of Christendom was stirred by the slogan of one of the most influential of the missionary organizations: "The evangelization of the world in this generation."

Second, these consecrated lives had borne fruit. Men were won to Christ, and the numbers of His followers were increased in this land and that. Churches were started, and Christian homes were begun. The contagion of the faith spread, from the pioneer missionary to those to whom he had given his life. From these two facts, the awakening of the churches of the West and the success of their efforts, came the additional fact that the Christian Church, alone of the institutions on the earth, on the very outbreak of the greatest war of mankind, was able to assemble together representative Christians not of the first but of at least the second and in some cases of the third and fourth generations from seventy-three nations. The gathering itself is, of course, not of primary importance: but as a symbol it is of the utmost significance, for it is evidence of the fact that the Christian Church has become a world-wide body.

Third, there lies behind this that which has been the source of the whole: the victorious Christ. It was not primarily the stirring accounts of strange lands, nor the lure of commerce, nor the general trend toward political expansion which produced the missionary enterprise of nineteenth-century Protestantism. In essence it was a reformation in the spiritual life

of the churches, which gave to them the vision of Christ reign-
ing in victory over the entire human race.

To this conception of world evangelism has been added a
vision of the influence of the Church upon all of society.
Although there are differences as to the way in which this
influence should be exerted, it is clear that the churches have
awakened to their responsibility for all men, and, equally
important, for all phases of life. The most comprehensive
expressions of this concern in recent times occurred with the
holding of the Oxford Conference on Life and Work in 1937
and the Madras Conference on the World Mission of the Church
in 1938. Here were elected representatives from the main non-
Roman churches of Christendom, gathered for the purpose of
considering, in addition to the evangelistic task of the Church,
its function in relation to economics, the state, education, the
development of community, rural problems and urban problems. A basic view of the relation of the Church to these issues
emerges from the reports of these meetings. They assert that
the Church has an inescapable responsibility for these areas of
life, discharged on the one hand by the effort to extend the
spirit of Christ through evangelism, and on the other by correlative efforts to offer guidance to Christians and to the nations
as a whole through constructive judgment. The actual response
of the churches to this comprehensive view has not been as
marked as the response to the vision of world evangelism. In the
matter of general social effectiveness there is much that is
lacking in contemporary church life; but that there has been
a renaissance of social vision and ethical responsibility, and
that this involves a comprehensive approach to society cannot
be denied.[17]

A final factor in the Church's assertion of its world mission

[17] James H. Nichols, Vol. I, pp. 195 ff.

must be noted. This is the conscious strategy of the churches to develop churches which are indigenous to their cultures. Although the beginnings of the missionary movement at times lacked grievously at this point, insisting upon the acceptance of customs which had only a local Western significance, in recent years the design has been altered. It has been recognized fully that Christianity could only flower in so far as it was given freedom to grow in forms which were native to the soil. This strategy has been of the utmost significance. It has provided for healthy growth in the younger churches. Had there been no yielding to the necessity of permitting indigenous growth, all growth whatsoever would doubtless have been stopped. Moreover, an indirect result of the policy has been of incalculable significance. The nineteenth century was the century of imperialism as well as of missions. The dominant political procedure was the imposition of one nation's will upon another nation. To this general trend, the practice of the churches offered a startling contrast. Here there was a demonstration of the sharing which is demanded of true community. Although one can find repeated violations of this general rule, nevertheless in the whole movement which gave rise to the "younger churches," there is exhibited not only the most enduring, but the sole major corrective to the dominant imperialism of the time. It was here that the Church gave the most convincing evidence of her disinterested love for peoples the world over.

3. THE VEHICLES OF THE REFORMATION

We have so far been dealing with general trends and directions which, all told, have spelled the existence of a far-reaching reformation. Although we have perforce noted various organized expressions of these movements, we have not attempted a description of the structure which has been evolved and within which this reformation is taking its course. But it is important to note that a comprehensive organization or rather series of organizations has arisen, which in various ways is giving expression to the ecumenical spirit, providing channels through which it may become effective, and supplying leadership for its continued development.

We shall be concerned with those organizations which have been created by, and are responsible to, the churches. This will place outside our purview all of those important agencies which are unofficial, and to which we have already made reference (pp. 82-3). Moreover, there are overlappings in function among these church-related organizations which defy a strict classification. Two examples may be cited. The Federal Council of the Churches of Christ in America is not directly concerned with foreign missions, although it does have relations with the churches abroad. On the other hand, it is directly concerned with the world mission of the Church as this refers to American society, and it is providing vigorous leadership in the matter of Christian unity in this country. The Foreign Missions Conference of North America, on the contrary, is concerned exclusively with the world mission of the Church in other lands, yet aggressively fosters a spirit of unity both in these lands and in the United States. We cannot, therefore, with absolute accuracy describe the structure of the ecumenical movement in terms of the two concepts of world mission and of unity which we have been using. Since, however, there is no other dividing line, we shall use these rough categories, mindful that there is frequently this altogether desirable overlapping. We shall be concerned with the ecumenical agencies in the United States and with the world ecumenical bodies.

The United States

(1) The missionary boards of the churches are basic to the ecumenical movement. They are the organizations which have kept the need for world evangelism before their constituent churches, and which have by conscious and concerted action kept the vision of Christ's Great Commission alive in them. They have year after year challenged the successive generations of young people to life service on the mission field, thus providing the personnel necessary for the growth of the entire missionary enterprise. They have maintained the educational program among their constituencies out of which the needed spiritual and financial support for this enterprise has come. Whether the missionary boards be for purposes of "foreign" or of "home" missions, they have been the chief means of awakening and maintaining the sense of responsibility to which all Christians are subject for the evangelization of the world.

The missionary boards have made a large direct contribution to the growth of a spirit of unity. The foreign boards are associated in the Foreign Missions Conference of North America, in which ninety-three of them plan through this permanent organization for united work. Allied to it is the Missionary Education Movement, maintaining the Friendship Press, through which basic educational materials ranging from pamphlets to full-size volumes, are unitedly planned and distributed. The "home," or national, boards are brought together in the Home Missions Council which, in addition to providing a means for joint planning and action, engages in a non-denominational program of home missions work on behalf of the boards which comprise it.

(2) The second part of the structure of the ecumenical move-

ment in the United States is formed by interchurch councils.[18] These are in essence co-operative agencies which have been formed by various churches for two purposes: to promote unity among the constituents, and to increase the effectiveness of their impact upon their respective communities. They are found at various levels, of which the first is geographic. Councils of churches are organized on a city, county, district and state basis. The second level is that of interest, of which the councils of religious education, Sunday-school associations and home missions councils are representative. The trend is in the direction of the organization of the inclusive type of council of churches; all told, at the present time, there are 535 councils in the country. In addition, there are large numbers of ministerial associations, of which several hundred have begun to assume the duties characteristic of the council of churches. These councils are to some degree carried on by voluntary work, but in the overwhelming majority have regular budgets and a paid staff. The significance of the entire structure lies in the fact that their central purpose is the promotion of unity and of vigor in the mission of the Church, and also in the further fact, as Paul Douglass has pointed out, that "they mean that a definite ecclesiastical structure is being evolved parallel and supplementary to the denominational system."[19]

(3) We may form a single category of a number of further organized expressions of the ecumenical movement. This is the development of consolidation in church organization itself. We have already indicated one aspect of it, namely, the full corporate union within denominational families and across those

[18] For a more complete analysis of ecumenical agencies in the United States from this point on, see H. Paul Douglass, Vol. IV, chap. 5, to which part of this treatment is heavily indebted.

[19] *Ibid.*, p. 182.

lines alike, of one or more churches. A second result of church consolidation has been the formation of community churches of different types. A minority of the present twenty-five hundred of these churches are strictly independent and nondenominational; the majority are united churches which have resulted from the merger of two or more local churches, maintaining relationships with either one or more of the denominations originally represented. No national, overall structure of these community churches has as yet been formed.

(4) A fourth category is found among the youth groups. First to be noted are the student movements. Originally the Y.M.C.A. and the Y.W.C.A. and the Student Volunteer Movement for Foreign Missions were the sole agencies in this field, and to them belongs the credit for significant pioneering at all points in the ecumenical reformation. The vision of world evangelism, of incisive social effectiveness, and of a united Church called forth large numbers of students who have taken, and today are taking, places of significant leadership in the churches. To their initial work has been added in recent years the strong and widespread efforts, particularly on the campuses of the large universities, of the church-related student foundations. Nearly all of the agencies engaged in student work are now united in the United Student Christian Council, in essence a federation. In the field of general youth work, the Young People's Society for Christian Endeavor was an early pioneer in co-operative work, and in more recent times the United Christian Youth Movement has sought to bring together all of the youth agencies on a comprehensive national basis. The working base of the United Christian Youth Movement is found in the city and state youth councils, which are part of the structure of interdenominational councils which we have already noted.

(5) The capstone of ecumenical structure in the United States is the Federal Council of the Churches of Christ in America. Parallel to it are seven other national ecumenical bodies: the Council of Church Boards of Education, the Foreign Missions Conference of North America, the Home Missions Council of North America, the International Council of Religious Education, the Missionary Education Movement of the United States and Canada, the United Council of Church Women and the United Stewardship Council. As their names indicate, however, their purposes are confined to a particular interest; the Federal Council alone is inclusive of the churches as such. As its name implies, it is a federation, bringing together the main churches on the American scene. It is governed by a constitution, fundamental power resting, however, with the churches which compose it. Its basic purposes are the achievement of greater evangelistic and social effectiveness on the part of the churches on the American scene, and the development of unity among them. The motivating philosophy is that unity is achieved most directly and vitally as churches *work* together on tasks which they have in common. Although its constitutional powers are limited, the Federal Council through the scope of its activities, the momentum of its prestige, and the wisdom of its leadership throughout its history has assumed a position today of inestimable importance in American church life.

It should be noted that further unification is projected. The eight agencies named above have formed numerous committees which over a period of years have been working at the problem of bringing these agencies into closer relationships. A plan is at present being studied by the constituent churches which would envisage "the creation of an inclusive co-operative agency to continue and extend" the work of the eight agencies, to be called the "National Council of the Churches of Christ in the United States of America." Whatever the eventual solution may be, it is important, and encouraging, to note the further development of unity in American ecumenical structure.

The world scene

Ecumenical structure on the world scene is understood through reference to two main organizations: the International Missionary Council, and the World Council of Churches which at present is still in the process of being formed.[20]

The International Missionary Council, in constitution a federation, is composed of two different types of agencies. On the one hand, its constituents are the co-operative associations of mission boards in the "sending" countries. Thus the American unit of the International Missionary Council is the Foreign Missions Conference; the British unit, the Conference of Missionary Societies in Great Britain and Ireland; the Dutch unit, the Netherlanddsche Zendings-Raad, etc. On the other hand, it is composed of the co-operative bodies, called National Christian Councils, in the "receiving" countries, that is, the countries of the "younger churches." These co-operative bodies are made up of the missions from the "older churches" in those lands and of the "younger churches" themselves. Thus the International Missionary Council has as its constituent

[20] The reader must be reminded of the limitation of our treatment to those agencies which are created by, and responsible to, the churches. Such important agencies in the history and the present working of the ecumenical movement as the World's Sunday School Association, the World's Alliance of Young Men's Christian Associations, the World's Young Women's Christian Association, the World's Student Christian Federation, and the World Alliance for International Friendship through the Churches are, therefore, omitted. The significance of their contribution, however, cannot be minimized. For a full discussion, see Henry Smith Leiper and Abdel R. Wentz, Vol. IV, chap. 3, p. I.

bodies agencies of the churches, namely, the foreign missionary boards and their co-operative agencies, as well as churches in their own right, namely, the "younger churches." It is the function of the International Missionary Council to promote the vigorous pursuit of world evangelism in its broadest sense, and to assist in unifying the many efforts of the churches to this end which are now in process. A series of great world conferences, in Edinburgh in 1910, in Jerusalem in 1928 and in Madras in 1938, representing both the "older churches" and the "younger churches," have been the source of immense inspiration and stimulation for the entire world missionary enterprise. Continuing processes of study, research, correlation and international travel have further developed its fundamental aims.

The significance of the International Missionary Council and all that it represents cannot be underestimated. It is of the highest importance for the future of the ecumenical reformation as a whole. Through it the vigor of the "younger churches" is felt upon the West: the demand for racial equality arising not only out of oppression but out of the clearly perceived requirements of the Gospel, and presented not only by a few leaders but by whole churches; the insistence upon, not merely Christian unity, but full organic union among the churches of Christendom; the assertion, from their vantage point as tiny minorities in an openly hostile country, of the utter necessity of evangelistic vigor; able and incisive leadership in regard to political and economical issues. Here indeed is light, of the kind that lightens the world. The International Missionary Council has not created the "younger churches," nor is it responsible for the life which they show, nor for all of the impact of this life upon the West. It is, however, the chief structural means by which this life is communicated to us, and

it provides the co-operative world structure by which it may
be heightened.

The World Council of Churches is the result of the fusion
of two movements, both originating in the twentieth century.
One of these movements was dedicated to a co-operative attack,
through the churches and on a world level, upon social evil.
It was the "Life and Work Movement," its central organization
being the Universal Christian Council for Life and Work. Two
world conferences were held under its leadership, at Stockholm
in 1925 and at Oxford in 1937. In the interim its work was
primarily that of maintaining contacts among the churches on
the major ethical issues of the day, and of developing a research bureau on these subjects, which was of large value to
the churches.

The second movement precursor to the World Council of
Churches was dedicated to an open discussion of the theological
issues which divide the churches, with a view to their solution.
It is the "Faith and Order Movement," and has also held two
world conferences, at Lausanne in 1927 and at Edinburgh in
1937. Like its sister movement, its work was directed in the
interim to the promotion of study among the churches of the
problems of their faith and order.

At the Oxford and the Edinburgh Conferences of 1937, a
plan was suggested, and in 1938 adopted, to form a World
Council of Churches. Each of the two movements had been
world wide, if not in the strictly geographical sense, in the
sense that together they included virtually all of the non-Roman
churches of Christendom. Although their approaches to the
problem of unity differed at the outset, the one assuming that
unity would grow around co-operative work in meeting a common ethical problem facing the churches, and the other maintaining that unity must be achieved by a direct confrontation

of the avowed theological differences among the churches, it became increasingly clear that these were not two separate methods, but different aspects of the same impulse. Consideration of ethical problems led inevitably to an examination of their theological significance, and discussion of theological problems revealed sources of disunity which were outside of the strictly theological realm. It was, moreover, clear that a more comprehensive approach to the entire problem was needed. The development according to interest, theological versus ethical, had proceeded with sufficient success to make it apparent that a serious attempt at unity would involve a world association of churches as churches.

The proposed World Council of Churches is a federation on a world scale. At the present writing ninety-six churches, including both the "older churches" of the West and the "younger churches," have subscribed to its constitution. It must be noted that inherently, although it is still in its infancy, the World Council of Churches is the most inclusive of the world ecumenical bodies, for it is composed of churches, rather than of missionary or other special agencies of the churches. The process of its organization proceeded from the initial proposals at the world conferences in 1937 to a "constitutional convention" at Utrecht in 1938. This was interrupted by the war, although throughout the war and because of its emergency demands, there were added almost insuperable tasks to the nascent organization.[21] The formal organization of the World Council will take place at the first Assembly which is scheduled for 1948.

It is obviously too early to evaluate the World Council of Churches. It is the most comprehensive of the agencies which have so far been proposed; because of its extensive wartime

[21] See further Charles W. Iglehart, Vol. IV, chap. 4, pt. II.

activities it has gained much experience and a large prestige. Though it comes at an advanced stage of a long development of ecumenical activity and organization, it is, however, certainly not the final embodiment of the ecumenical spirit. Yet that it is the most hopeful symbol and organized expression of the ecumenical reformation, there can be no doubt.

4. THE SIGNIFICANCE OF THE REFORMATION

Even though we may go back a century and more for the first beginnings of the ecumenical reformation, found in the awakening which brought forth the modern missionary enterprise, it is a movement which is still in its infancy. The primary evidence of this is the distance which the movement has still to go to reach completion. Although the longing for unity and the vision of the universal reign of Christ are shared literally by millions of Christians, it is apparent to even the most casual observer that the Church is far from unified, and that the world is not possessed by Christ. It is even almost absurd, in the face of our hundreds of separated and bickering congregations and their larger organizations, to think of the day when they may all exhibit the unity of the true Body. And in a world which hardly has the strength to heal the still open sores of war—which the Church did not prevent and which it did little to alleviate, in spite of its immense relief programs— and which in cowering fear already thinks of a third world war, it is all but a hollow mockery to speak of the universal reign of the Prince of Peace. It would not be so were we in the presence of a world body of Christians, however small and overwhelmed, who were exercising their strength to the full. But we are not. Although throughout the war and by means of its pressures, God raised up in the Church new life which one would not have thought possible, there still remain vast blocs of it which are inert. Of these none is so conspicuous as that in the United States. Possessed of wealth, manpower, leadership and freedom to a degree not paralleled by any other section of Christendom, the vast majority of the membership of the churches in this country still await the awakening which will send them forth with power on their mission in the world. Clearly, the ecumenical reformation is still in its earliest days.

The fact is also borne out by the lack of well-defined goals. This is particularly true in the assertion of the unity of the Church. The concept of the world mission of the Church, involving world evangelism and a comprehensive, penetrating effect upon society, is generally enough accepted. But there is no statement of "the ecumenical goal" in relation to Christian unity which is not challenged by wide numbers of people.[22] Although, as we have noted, mutual recognition among Christians and churches is basic and although at the present time federation seems to be the most generally accepted form of co-working, these are not considered final by anyone. Beyond these there stand the possibilities of federal union and of corporate union; but these are, so far as a widespread adoption of them is concerned, but proposals around which debate is rife. The churches may speak now, as they have always spoken, of the unity of the Body of Christ; but the translation of this into a structural goal is a matter for future determination.

Practical importance

Although we are but in the beginning of the movement, part of its significance may nevertheless be determined. First of all,

[22] For a discussion of various aspects of the problem see John A. Mackay and John C. Bennett, Vol. IV, chap. 2, pts. 1-2.

the ecumenical reformation is of immense practical importance. We have noted the fact that it is in the full sense of the word a movement. It is not confined to any single agency or "school"; it appears, as we have seen, in a multitude of different forms. It is not dependent upon the genius of a few leaders; it rather is evolved from the joint prayers and thinking and work of thousands. This means that it is a reformation which is dependent for its very existence, to say nothing of its future effectiveness, upon the support of the general membership of the churches. It is a movement which, in its essence, has a direct relevance to every communicant and minister. The unity of the churches cannot come about unless the unity of the Church arises in force through the body of the people. The mission of the churches cannot be fulfilled unless it is embodied in the vocation of every person who calls himself a Christian. The practical importance of the ecumenical reformation lies first in the fact that it is above all a people's reformation.

It is also to be found in its results. It is axiomatic that the unity of the churches will, even by two or three times, increase their effectiveness. The exclusiveness, inefficiency and confusion of tongues to which we have already had reference will be, and indeed to some extent already are, corrected, with the result that a genuine community may be about its business with less waste and greater impact. The matter is both spiritual and organizational. As Jesus has told us, and all of our political and psychological experience has confirmed, a house which is divided within itself is weakened internally: the strength resulting from a unified spirit within the Body of Christ is incalculable. No less so are the organizational benefits, for in the unity which is being hammered out, and in that greater measure which must come, is to be found a large saving of time and energy and money. A single example will suffice. During the war, the Federal Council of Churches was the representative for the Protestant churches with government on a number of issues. It was only through such a united voice that the churches could be heard in Washington at all. If, however, each church had been permitted to send its own representative, it takes only a small imagination to calculate the immense expenditure which would have been involved. The practical effect of unity cannot be denied.

World civilization

Our world, we said, is characterized by the substitution of a mechanical for a spiritual unity. There is no toughness of spirit which holds the mechanical parts of our world society together. It is at this point that the ecumenical reformation carries its largest promise for the life of mankind, for it is the single movement which claims to lay, and in any appreciable degree has laid, the spiritual basis upon which the nations may live together. The pursuit of the world mission of Christ, and the grand strategy whereby the awakening to his Spirit has been allowed to develop freely and with roots which have drawn strength from the different cultures, is our one ultimate hope. The matter must not be romanticized. It must be recognized, for instance, that the church of the nation with which the United States finds it most difficult to live in harmony, namely, Russia, is not within the ecumenical fellowship, and so far as one can judge, is largely under the control of the Russian government. It may be that the establishment of a spiritual world unity may fail at this crucial point. Moreover, the very numerical weakness of the Church in some lands, as in China, and its sterility, as in the United States, may mean that it cannot generate sufficient vitality to alter the course of political events. We cannot afford an undue optimism. The fact, however, still stands that it is in the ecumenical reformation, especially that aspect of it which has asserted the world mission of the Church, that any progress has been made at all. Whatever accomplishments may or may not be possible for it in the immediate future, it is the means by which the reign of the universal Christ is established in the world.

The Church

The ultimate significance of the ecumenical reformation, however, lies in the fact that it recaptures for our time the basic New Testament concept of the Church. This is indeed the reason why it is of importance at all. For if it did not seek to recover that which was the intent of the Lord for his followers, it could have no meaning for the Christian and could not prevail over the world rulers of this darkness.

We may take three New Testament concepts as symbolic of the message which it has concerning the nature of the Church. The first of these is the Great Commission: "Go therefore and make disciples of all nations, baptizing them in the name of the Father and of the Son and of the Holy Spirit, teaching them to observe all that I have commanded you" (Matthew 28:19-20). The debate as to whether these words were actually spoken by Jesus need not detain us. They are thoroughly consistent with the figure of Jesus. They are implied by his teachings as these are presented in the Gospels; they are, moreover, in full harmony with the life work and the writings of Paul. They were for the early Christians, as for us, a command of the Lord and as such formed an integral part of the conception which these early Christians, to whom we owe the gospels themselves, had of the Church whose life they began. In it was involved a vision of a world mission; in it was contained the conviction that no part of life should be left unredeemed. As Professor Latourette has pointed out, it is important that it comes at the close of the gospel which contains the Sermon on the Mount. There has not been such a sweeping vision of the mission of the Church in all of Christian literature.

The second concept is given to us by Jesus' prayer: "That they may all be one . . . so that the world may believe." Again we have a concept fully in harmony with Jesus' life, implied in his command to love, and enjoined, albeit in different words, by Paul. This is the vision of unity. It is, however, not a unity which is desired for aesthetic reasons; the fervor of Jesus' prayer was not born out of a Greek desire for proportion. This is unity which is desired for a purpose. The reply of Jesus that "a house divided against itself cannot stand," is here translated into the desire of his soul, that the world might not be confused, but might believe.

The third concept gathers up the preceding two. It is the concept of St. Paul that the Church is the Body of Christ. His equivalent for this phrase in passive terms was "you are God's temple"; his equivalent for it in active terms was "we are ambassadors for Christ." By this he meant to convey that in the company of the redeemed, the Spirit of Jesus, not dead but living, moves to animate the countless hands and feet which were to take the place of his hands and his feet. That this was a single body is revealed by his indignant question: "Is Christ divided?" In Paul's concept of the Body of Christ is summed up the dynamic unity of loving spirit which is distinctive of the entire New Testament concept of the Church.

It is this concept which the ecumenical reformation recaptures for our day. World evangelism and world social mission; spiritual unity which contains the power and honesty for overt expression; above all a new vision. For its motivating power and its highest loyalty we may turn again to that group of young Christians who met so hopefully on the eve of the war, confessing with them as with the entire movement: *Christus Victor*.

4

THE TASK AHEAD

1. The call to evangelism. 2. The call to comprehensive social effectiveness. 3. The call to unity. 4. The responsibility of the local congregation.

WE have seen that the fundamental characteristic of our time is that contemporary society depersonalizes men, robbing them of their full stature as men. We have seen further that, historically considered, the function of the Church is to be found in providing men with the Christian gospel, the aim of which is the restoration in man of the image of God: that the function of the Church is evangelism, and that there proceeds from this the constant and varied efforts of the Church, both directly and indirectly, to alter its surrounding civilization in the interests of justice. We have seen that the dominant feature of modern church life is that it is in the midst of the ecumenical reformation, which has as its two poles the assertion of the world mission and the unity of the Church. What does this mean for the present and future task of the Church?

The primary and most urgent answer to this question is in the need of the Church as a whole for a rediscovery of the Bible and of prayer. These are perennial needs, for all Christians and at all times. They come now, however, with a special insistence. The way ahead is not clear. How shall we rid the churches and the world of the power of color caste? How shall we develop the life of the nations with each other so that we may at last live in peace with one another? How shall we distribute the world's goods so that men at least will not starve and die of diseases which could be prevented? Or, in a different context, though we see clearly the demand for Christian unity and have had some experience in developing it, how shall we proceed from here? If federation appears to be workable but incomplete, to what other structure shall we turn? Above all, what means can we use to insure that there is that basic humility which will leave the judgment of differences to God, and proceed on the basis alone of devotion to Him? The way is not clear for us. On every hand there is revolution: in political life in China and India, in economic life in the United States, throughout the entire social fabric of Europe, in the Church. It is a time when God is working out new patterns for His children, and their outline is not apparent.

On every hand we hear the cry for power. The world is frightened by the physical power which is in its hands: the amassed wealth and industry and populations which, capped by the availability of atomic power, are held in equilibrium by the merest threads of fear and self-interest. Men long for spiritual power. There is a deep understanding, both conscious and intuitive, that there is needed a force which will bend men's wills into moral living.

Where but in prayer and in the Bible can guidance and power be found? If God exists at all, it is through communication with Him, that kind of communication which probes the depths of the human spirit and lifts it to the heights, that His purposes can be known. This does not just "happen." We understand that the grace of God toward men cannot be forced, and that His movements are in His own time and in

His own ways. Yet they cannot, as the teachings of Jesus and the experience of the Church well testify, become movements at all unless there is a seeking after Him. "Because of his importunity he will give him whatever he needs" (Luke 11:8). Yet communication with God is not alone, and probably not, primarily, a matter of mystical contact, on whatever level that may be maintained. It is of the very essence of the Gospel that God *has made* Himself known to us, and that with power. The Bible is the ultimate source of our knowledge: ultimate in the sense that it is the Bible which is the standard and the judge of all related Christian experience, and ultimate in the sense that here the final revelation of God has been given to us. Knowledge of the Bible does not mean mere knowledge of the words contained in it, though one must hesitate long before assuming that any of its words do not have imperative significance for us. Fundamental knowledge of the Bible, however, means immersion of one's mind in its central message about man and God and the relation between them. It is from this immersion in Biblical truth that prayer takes on its meaning. The attitude and the techniques of prayer, which are of large psychological significance, may be learned from other sources, but the content of prayer, the knowledge of the God whom we address, comes from the Bible. This is our most urgent task. Before all else, we must engage in the disciplines of Biblical study and prayerful waiting from which, if the Promise means anything at all, will come that wisdom and power and forgiveness whereby our lives may be managed.

With this ever in the forefront, we may suggest that the task of the Church may be stated in four imperatives:

(1) *The call to evangelism.* The Church is called with an insistence which cannot be denied to a new life of evangelism. This call issues from two sources. On the one hand, it is pre-

sented by the nature of our contemporary world. If depersonal-ization contains in it any challenge at all, it is the challenge to restore these personalities which are being stifled and torn apart. This restoration must have the power to break through materialistic obsessions and the domination of our lives by organized groups and mass minds; it must have the scope to provide our world civilization and the various cultures within it with an underlying spiritual unity; it must have the depth to plumb the human consciousness so as to make its normal tensions creative and not destructive. Jesus, it has been said, was either the great deceiver or the greatly deceived. Christians believe that he was neither; that he is rather the power of God, and that in the spread of his reign, through the work of evangelism, is to be found that basic cure for our sickness, namely, obedience to the will of God and entrance into eternal life, out of which other solutions may be wrought. This is the other source of the call to evangelism. It comes from the very character of the Christian faith, and the nature of the Christian Church. It is the soul of the world, established by God to bring light into darkness. The perils of our world and the nature of the Church insist that there must be a rebirth of evangelistic endeavor. This is the first and all-important task of the Chris-tian in the world.

We are presented, moreover, with a challenge to a specific evangelistic strategy. During the past century there has been considerable success with regard to the evangelization of in-dividuals. Much of American Protestantism and virtually all of the "younger churches," excepting certain sections of those in India and Africa, have been the result of the conversion of individuals, one by one. This we must continue to do, for ultimately the healing and with it the dawning of new life must take place in the individual soul. Yet we live in an age of group consciousness, in which we think in groups and act in groups. As Richard Niebuhr has well pointed out,[1] the Gospel must be announced, both in terms of prophetic judgment and in terms of redemptive power, to groups. We have but little historical experience, and almost none in the modern period, upon which to rely for such an approach. Yet the necessity of pioneering in this regard is unmistakable. It is a fallacy, as our experience and social investigation alike point out, to suppose that we may effectively deal one by one with persons whose lives are in fact controlled by groups. These are the modern mountains which we must have the faith to move; for upon this depends the life of multitudes now held prisoners by the powers of our social order.

Although the need for pioneering is obvious as we proceed and expand our evangelistic efforts, we are supplied with some basically important clews. These are given to us by the reformation through which we are passing, and indicate that evangelism can no longer be a sporadic effort of now this group and now that, the one offering this gospel and the other offering a different one. Nor can evangelism be confined to a single people. The ecumenical reformation means that we must concentrate the full impact of the Christian experience of the various traditions and races and nations upon each specific situation. The Gospel must be presented as coming from the *whole* Church to the individual and the group to which it is addressed. A single example will suffice to indicate what is meant. There is hardly a large university, and increasingly few small colleges, which will grant to one of the student movements in this country, that is, to one of the church-related movements or to the Y.M.C.A. or Y.W.C.A., the privilege of addressing the entire campus on behalf of the Christian faith.

[1] Richard Niebuhr, Vol. III, p. 128.

Rather than be subjected to a sectarian claim, administrations by legal action and students by the quality of their response demand a united voice. More than this, it has been the experience of those engaged in this work that a "team" representing not only the different churches, but also representing Christians of other lands are of incalculably greater effectiveness in engaging students' attention. This is important not only as indicating the general temper of the time. It is important because of the crucial strategic nature of student evangelism. Democracy rests upon an educated populace, and looks, by and large, to its educated citizens for leadership. It requires but little imagination to see the imperative character of doing all within the power of human effort to insure that those graduating from the institutions of higher learning are Christians. Yet unless the Church follows the lead already supplied it by the ecumenical reformation through which it is now going, this will not happen. Here as elsewhere, a united voice and the full impact of the experience of the ages and of the nations are required. This is part of the meaning of ecumenical evangelism.

The other aspect of it is contained in the heightened demand for a world evangelistic vision. The existence of "younger churches" does not lessen the demand upon us to help with the evangelistic task throughout the world. Two of these, those in China and Japan, have been so weakened in their material resources by the war, that it is only by a supreme triumph of the spirit that they continue to maintain a vigorous life. On every hand, the "younger churches" are a minority of all but overwhelming proportions. By their own admission and urging, missionaries and more missionaries are needed. It is no reflection upon the superb efforts of the foreign boards to say that the current demand for a thousand volunteers for foreign service is but the merest beginning. Nor is the evangelistic task in this country less demanding. The Church here, although not in the same drastic proportion as in the lands of the "younger churches," is also a minority, and if one subtract the nominal Christians from the reported church roles, its minority status becomes the more alarming. By whatever standard, whether this be numbers or influence, the world calls for an evangelistic effort of world-wide scope. And without it, the ecumenical reformation which offers such large hope for us will unquestionably die. In the demand for a unified and a world-wide resurgence of evangelism we have the fundamental clews as to the specific nature of our task.

(2) *The call to comprehensive social effectiveness.* Logically, this is derived from the call to evangelism with which we are confronted. Just as social transformation historically has proceeded from the basic function of the Church in making the Gospel live among men, so in our current scene the logical sequence of our challenge is directed. Yet we must not conclude from this that we may proceed with evangelism and then *later* attend to the correction of injustice. Men want justice now. Just as evangelism itself must be carried on in reference to the group consciousness which controls individual lives, so there must be a simultaneous effort to alter the structure of society in order that human beings may find a full life. The direction which our efforts must take are again already discernible. Inasmuch as the structure of society depersonalizes the individual, the social judgments of the Church, its efforts at legislative reform on both the national and international level, its relations with labor and with management and its impact upon racial prejudice must be directed toward the correction of this basic evil. This, however, cannot be a matter of easygoing evolution. The time is short; our society is close

to the end result of its mechanization, and is threatened with collapse. Whether this will be violent or will come about through economic paralysis at home and political stalemate internationally cannot be foreseen. The need, however, for immediate action is urgent. As we have seen, the response of the Church to this need must be in terms of its universal responsibility. It cannot remain true to its character and ally itself with one group to the unjust expense of another. Its accountability is to God, who is the Father of all; and it must be responsive to need wherever this is found. This is also to say that the response of the Church must be comprehensive in character: it cannot be content with one segment of life, or one group in society. There is in the ecumenical reformation no room for the "individual" or the "social" gospel. The assertion of ecumenical Christianity is that there is one Gospel, and that it is relevant to all of life and to all of the relationships of life. And as there is one Gospel, so there is one Church. The impact of the Christian minority upon the towering concentrations of power will come to naught unless this is directed by a united strategy. No less than the call to. evangelism, the call to social effectiveness is a demand for a comprehensive attack, carried on simultaneously with its evangelistic work, and exhibiting the full strength of a united effort.

(3) *The call to unity*. The urgency of unity is clear. By what means may we progress further along the road? We venture to suggest three:

First, through all of the humility of spirit which we may gain from the study of Biblical truth and from the disciplines of prayer and from the depths of fellowship, we must maintain that mutual recognition of one another as Christians which is at the base of all Christian unity. This is the prime spiritual condition of all further advance, as it has been of all progress to this time. At root, it is the recognition that God and not man is the judge, that the conceptions of our limited minds cannot be regarded as ultimate Truth. It is the recognition that the exclusiveness which because of doctrinal or Biblical or traditional disagreement prohibits fellowship, whether in common work or in the sanctity of the Lord's Table, is contrary to the will of Christ. This is not a condition which we can create by the decisions of our minds; it is an inward disposition, born of devotion to the Father and the knowledge that in Him alone is truth.

Second, we may advance through the systematic exploitation of commitments already made. Virtually all of the major denominations in this country and the world are members of one or another of the co-operative organizations which form the structure of the ecumenical movement. As such they have made commitments as regards co-operative work or study or worship or all three. These commitments should be exploited on every level of the life of the denomination. Is the foreign board of the church a member of the Foreign Missions Conference? Let it act in unison on the foreign field, and let it act at home in co-operation with other churches also members of the Foreign Missions Conference in promotion of the missionary enterprise. Is the church a member of the International Council of Religious Education? Let it use the educational materials in its Sunday schools and youth groups which have been worked out with the wisdom of joint planning. Is it a member of the Federal Council of Churches? Let it join with other churches in programs of united evangelism, of united recruiting for the ministry, of united social action—all of which are activities of the Federal Council. Is the church a member of the World Council of Churches? Let it engage in earnest discussions with the other churches in order to transcend its theological differences with them, and let it participate unitedly in the relief work which will be for so long into the future an important part of the work of the World Council. Commitments already made should be exploited to the full. This will require study to ascertain what the commitments are, and how they may be exploited. But the systematic pursuit of this course from the national through the regional to the local levels of each denomination would not only consolidate the gains already made, but provide the spirit and the experience of unity from which advance may be expected.

Third, there is immediate need for pioneering. Let us recall three problems as illustrations. The first is theological in character. The single, most difficult theological problem preventing the unity of the churches is the question of the ordination of the ministery. We need not discuss the various issues contained in it. Suffice it to say that the center of the problem is: by what power is the minister ordained as a minister and from whom does he receive his authority, from congregation, presbytery or episcopate? This in turn raises questions as to the nature of the Church: wherein is the real continuity which the Church has from the apostolic times? To date no satisfactory solution has been found to the question, and churches are prevented from intercommunion and organic union alike because of this fact. Here is an area for pioneering, calling for the most creative and humble of the minds of the Church. The second is organizational. We have referred to the current debate on the wisdom of full corporate union for the churches of Christendom. This debate raises the general question: what form will the organized expression of Christian unity take? What will be the next steps, and what will be the ultimate goal? Here is a call for theologians, organizers and sociologists alike, for the further unification of agencies as vast in their sum total as the churches will raise all of these problems in their most acute form. The third problem is primarily sociological. The churches, as we have indicated, partake of the characteristics of their surrounding cultures. For this reason they are divided not only denominationally but in terms of class and of nation and of race as well. How may these tenacious divisions be healed? There is compelling force in the truth which Richard Niebuhr has put clearly for us,[2] that the Church must be the representative to mankind of the love of Christ, exhibiting that love in its corporate life. Yet here we are not ambassadors but traitors, and we have succumbed to the attraction of the foreign land. To recover the true loyalty which will overcome these divisions will require pioneering of the most creative type.

(4) *The responsibility of the local congregation.* We have so far been speaking in general terms. There can be no escaping the fact, however, that there will be no Christian advance, either in evangelism or social effectiveness or unity unless it is rooted in the conviction and work of the congregations. Our task ahead may, therefore, be stated in even more specific terms.

Each Christian must be an evangelist, and must seek to insure that the congregation of which he is a member is awakened to its evangelistic task in the community. As did the early Christians, he must use every opportunity—on the job, during the contacts of leisure hours, and particularly in his home—to exemplify and to tell men of the Gospel of Christ. The congregation must not rest until Christ reigns throughout the community. The congregation must press for a reawakening within the denomination. The individual and the congregation and the denomination, using every resource at their command—personal witness, public address, the press, radio—

[2] Vol. III, pp. 130 ff.

must address not only individuals but also the groups with which they come into contact. Individual Christians, congregations and denominations alike must support their mission boards. Here is the established and effective means of world evangelism. Increased support here is both evidence and fruit of evangelistic vigor throughout.

The congregation must assume the brunt of the social responsibility of the churches. The practice of passing a stern resolution about social evil and then doing nothing is notorious. Specific action, toward these bad working conditions, this unjust strike, that restrictive covenant, and political corruption is imperative. This is not to neglect the functions of the larger bodies of the churches. These are also important; but they are impotent unless they are the expression of aggressive and ethically disciplined congregations.

It is through the congregation that unity will ultimately be achieved among the churches. Where else can a Negro church become united with a white church to show forth the unity of the Body unless at the local level? How can legal enactments permitting intercommunion and corporate union be effective unless they rest upon the love of people in the congregation for their neighboring Christians? What force will make the commitments into which we have already entered effective unless it is the active will of those in the local churches? The denominations through the decisions of the top councils cannot make an effective united evangelistic appeal. It is up to the congregations to band together in the community to do that. The resolution of the Federal Council of Churches denouncing segregation in the churches cannot produce interracial fellowship. Only the local congregations can do that. This is the point of ultimate responsibility. The rebirth to which the Church is summoned cannot transpire unless it is through the energies of the *people* united in a community of true love.

The task ahead may be summarized in a sentence. It is that of furthering with every ounce of spiritual energy which we may be given and with all of the wisdom which we possess the ecumenical reformation already started. In this reformation is the primacy of the Gospel, the world vision of its need and effectiveness, the unity germane to the Spirit of Christ, which is alike demanded of us by the condition of the world and by the will of God.

SUBJECTS AND MEMBERSHIP OF
THE COMMISSIONS

COMMISSION I-A

VOLUME I. *The Challenge of Our Culture*

CLARENCE T. CRAIG: *Chairman*
JAMES LUTHER ADAMS
ELMER J. F. ARNDT
JOHN K. BENTON
CONRAD BERGENDOFF
BUELL G. GALLAGHER
H. C. GOERNER
GEORGIA HARKNESS
JOSEPH HAROUTUNIAN

WALTER M. HORTON
JAMES H. NICHOLS
VICTOR OBENHAUS
WILHELM PAUCK
ROLLAND W. SCHLOERB
EDMUND D. SOPER
ERNEST F. TITTLE
AMOS N. WILDER
DANIEL D. WILLIAMS

COMMISSION I-B

VOLUME II. *The Church and Organized Movements*

The Pacific Coast Theological Group:

RANDOLPH C. MILLER: *Chairman*
JAMES C. BAKER
EUGENE BLAKE
KARL MORGAN BLOCK
JOHN WICK BOWMAN
ELLIOTT VAN N. DILLER

GALEN FISHER
ROBERT M. FITCH
BUELL G. GALLAGHER
CYRIL GLOYN
GEORGE HEDLEY

JOHN KRUMM

PIERSON PARKER

MORGAN ODELL

CLARENCE REIDENBACH

JOHN SKOGLUND

DWIGHT SMITH

FREDERIC SPIEGELBERG

EVERETT THOMSON

ELTON TRUEBLOOD

AARON UNGERSMA

HUGH VERNON WHITE

LYNN T. WHITE

GEORGE WILLIAMS

Guests of the Theological Group:

JOHN H. BALLARD

THEODORE H. GREENE

EDWARD OHRENSTEIN

EDWARD LAMBE PARSONS

HOWARD THURMAN

STACY WARBURTON

FREDERICK WEST

COMMISSION II

VOLUME III. *The Gospel, The Church and The World*

KENNETH SCOTT LATOURETTE: *Chairman*

EARL BALLOU

JOHN C. BENNETT

NELS F. S. FERRÉ

JOSEPH FLETCHER

HERBERT GEZORK

EDWARD R. HARDY, JR.

ELMER HOMRIGHAUSEN

STANLEY HOPPER

JOHN KNOX

BENJAMIN MAYS

WILLIAM STUART NELSON

RICHARD NIEBUHR

JUSTIN NIXON

NORMAN PITTENGER

JAMES McD. RICHARDS

LUMAN J. SHAFER

PAUL SCHERER

WYATT A. SMART

GEORGE F. THOMAS

FRANK WILSON

COMMISSION III

VOLUME IV. *Toward World-wide Christianity*

O. FREDERICK NOLDE: *Chairman*

EDWIN R. AUBREY

ROSWELL P. BARNES

JOHN C. BENNETT

Arlo A. Brown
E. Fay Campbell
J. W. Decker
H. Paul Douglass
Charles Iglehart
F. Ernest Johnson
Charles T. Leber
Henry Smith Leiper

John A. Mackay
Elmore N. McKee
Lawrence Rose
Stanley Rycroft
Matthew Spinka
A. L. Warnshuis
A. R. Wentz
Alexander C. Zabriskie

Volume V. *What Must the Church Do?*

Robert S. Bilheimer

COMPLETE INDEX
VOLUMES I-V
THE INTERSEMINARY SERIES

[The volume number appears in bold-face roman numerals; the page number in light-face type.]

~~~~~~

125

Humanism, **I**—4, 163, 173; **II**—23,
30, 167 ff.; **III**—104, 194;
IV—9, 30
anthropocentric, **II**—38 ff.
ethical, **II**—169 f.
pragmatic, **II**—167 ff.
Humanitarianism, **III**—103 t.
Hutchins, Robert M., **II**—171
Huxley, Aldous, **III**—68
quoted, **I**—152, 161
Hysteria, **I**—113, 114, 116

"I Am" movement, **II**—181, 182,
201
Idealism
irrelevant, **I**—190; **II**—17
relation of, to the practical, **III**
—176 ff.
Iglehart, Charles W., **IV**—ix, xv
Illiteracy, religious, **III**—99 f., 143,
144
Immigration, **IV**—7, 178, 179
Immortality, **III**—7 ff., 70 ff., 76 ff.;
V—33 f.
Imperialism
Christian, **I**—84 f., 93 ff.; **V**—42
political and economic, **I**—43 ff.,
46, 179; **V**—91
Impersonal relations, **I**—171 ff.
India, **IV**—112
Individualism
false, **IV**—76
in the Reformation and Renais-
sance, **III**—193, 194
and religion, **III**—172, 173
Inductive approach to resistance,
II—19 ff.
Industrial foundations, **II**—115
Industrial Workers of the World,
II—57 f.
Industrialism, **I**—11 ff., 142 f., 148,
177; **II**—160; **III**—195; **V**—3

Infinity vs. eternity, **I**—20
Information, sources of, on Chris-
tian wartime activities, **IV**—
122 f.
Insanity, **I**—111 ff.
Institutionalizing process, **IV**—170
ff.
institutional mindedness, **IV**—
173 f.
Institutions, churches as, **V**—69 ff.,
76 ff.
Integrity, moral, **II**—239 ff.
Intellectualism, **III**—5
Interchurch councils, **IV**—181 ff.,
192 f.; **V**—94
Intercommunication, **V**—18
Interdenominationalism; *see* Co-
operation, interdenominational
Interdependence of society, **V**—
17 f.
International Christian Press and
Information Service, **IV**—123
International Missionary Council,
II—232; **IV**—71, 84, 88, 89 ff.,
103, 216, 217; **V**—85, 97 f.
Constitution of, **IV**—251 ff.
message of Ad Interim Commit-
tee of, **IV**—242 ff.
International Round Table, **IV**—
133
Internationalism (*see also* Ecumen-
ical movement)
Christianity and, **I**—173 f.
fraternal, **II**—149 f.
in government, inadequacy of,
IV—140
Protestant, **III**—101 f.
and world peace, **IV**—91, 126 ff.
Interprofessional Association, **II**—
66
Irresponsibility, **III**—115 f.
religious, **III**—120 ff.

Resources for Christianity—*Continued*
methods of assessing, II—18 ff.
in missions, II—231 ff.
in non-Christian religions, II—220 ff.
Responsibility
apostolic, III—126 ff.
Christian, for society, I—195 ff.; III—111 ff., 177 ff.; IV—74 ff., 153; V—54 f., 60, 61, 90, 115
distribution of, IV—229
ecumenical, IV—85 f.
to God, III—117 ff.
government, IV—149 ff.
of local congregation, V—118 f.
meaning of, III—114 ff.
pastoral, III—129 f.
pioneering, III—130 ff.
power and, I—58 f., 71, 72
social, I—195 ff.; III—212 ff.; IV—77, 141 f., 229; V—60, 114 f., 119
Resurrection, III—7 ff., 76 ff.
Revivalist Christianity, II—33
Revivals, religious, IV—6, 8, 174 f.
Reynolds, Robert R., II—91
Ritual
lodge, II—143
loss of, I—147 ff.; V—15
Robey, Ralph, on fascism, II—83 f.
Roman Catholic Church, I—125, 179; II—8, 10; IV—30 ff.; V—65 f.
attendance at, II—142
attitude of, to communism and fascism, II—18 f., 74
doctrine of, IV—37 f.
ecumenical unity and, IV—44 f.
education in, IV—36 f.
Roman Catholic Church—*Continued*
expansion of, III—93 f., 95 f., 101
immigration and, IV—7, 11
man's possibility in eyes of, III—65
membership in, IV—13
and the papacy, IV—33 ff.
and politics, IV—37
possible decline of, III—106 f.
Protestantism and, III—108, 139 f.; IV—37 f., 227 f.
reform in, IV—31 f.
stand of, against Nazism, IV—114 f.
and the state, IV—35 f.
U.S.S.R. and, III—146
Romanticism, I—141 f., 144; V—14
Rootlessness, I—149 ff.; V—15 f.
Rugg, Harold, II—169
Rukeyser, M. S., quoted, I—158
Rule of Benedict, V—46
Rumanian Orthodox Church, IV—26
Russell, Bertrand, I—43
Russell, William, on technocracy, II—95
Russia; *see* Soviet Union
Russian Orthodox Church, IV—21 ff., 108
Rycroft, W. Stanley, IV—xi, xv

Sacraments
intercommunion of churches on, IV—189 f.
restoration of, III—53 f., 217
of Roman Catholic Church, IV—38
St. John's College, II—171
"St. Thomas" Christians, I—85

Salvation, **III**—197, 199; **IV**—16

Sanderson, Ross W., quoted, **IV**—208

Scapegoating, **I**—76, 77, 191, 192; **II**—85

Scherer, Paul, **III**—xi

Schlatter, Michael, **IV**—5

Schmucker, Samuel, **IV**—100, 175 f., 188

Schizophrenia, **I**—111, 112, 115

School, religious education and, **I**—67 f.

Science

expansion of, **II**—159 f.

moral concern of, **II**—44

in philosophy, **I**—143 ff.

in practice, **I**—142 f.

religion and, **III**—171 f.

and scientism, **II**—158 f., 164

and warfare, **I**—47 f.

Scientism, **II**—37 f., 158 ff.

Sectionalism, **IV**—179

Sects, **IV**—1 f., 11, 55 f.

Secularism, **II**—23, 24, 30, 35, 49 ff.; **III**—47 f.

in the Church, **I**—168 ff.; **II**—145 ff.; **III**—145, 166; **V**—72

of the family, **III**—174

scientism and, **II**—158 ff.

of vocation, **III**—194

of Western society, **I**—140 ff.

Segal, Eugene, on Nationalists, **II**—91 f.

Serbian Church, **IV**—26 f.

Service clubs, **II**—136 f., 141, 148, 149, 152

Service to others, **III**—203 f., 218 f.

Sex

and the Church, **I**—185 f.

escapism and, **I**—127

Shafer, Luman J., **III**—xi

Shaftesbury, A. A. C., **V**—50

Sheldon, W. H., quoted, **I**—130 f.

Shotwell, James T.

on secularism, **III**—47

on total war, **I**—48

Silliman, Benjamin, **II**—159

Sin

and redemption, **III**—62 ff., 79

vocation and, **III**—196 f., 201, 206

Six Pillars of Peace, **IV**—131, 132, 150, 164

Slave Trade, **I**—90

Slavery

abolition of, in England, **V**—50

Church division on, **III**—141

Smith, Dwight C., **II**—x

Smith, Gerald L. K., **II**—13, 72, 91

Sobornost, doctrine of, **III**—52; **IV**—64; **V**—69

Social agencies, council of, **II**—117 f.

Social Democratic party (German), **II**—50

Social ills, **I**—15 ff., 30, 36, 61, 68

Social gospel, **I**—195 ff.; **II**—71, 109 f.; **III**—129, 156

Social Justice and Economic Reconstruction, **IV**—130, 150

Social Service State, **II**—119 f.

Social tensions, **III**—186 ff.

"Social uplift" movements, **II**—109 f.

Social work; *see* Welfare work

Socialist Labor party, **II**—54 f.

Socialist party (U.S.A.), **II**—53 f.

Society for the Promotion of Christian Union, **IV**—175 ff.

Sociological differences among American churches, **IV**—10 f.